THE IRISH UPRISING, 1914–21

uncovered editions

Series editor: Tim Coates

Other titles in the series

The Amritsar Massacre: General Dyer in the Punjab, 1919

The Boer War: Ladysmith and Mafeking, 1900

British Battles of World War I, 1914–15

The British Invasion of Tibet: Colonel Younghusband, 1904

D Day to VE Day, 1944–45: General Eisenhower's report on the invasion of Europe

Defeat at Gallipoli: The Dardanelles Commission Part II, 1915–16

Florence Nightingale and the Crimea, 1854–55

John Profumo and Christine Keeler, 1963

The Judgement of Nuremberg, 1946

Lord Kitchener and Winston Churchill: The Dardanelles Commission Part I, 1914–15

The Loss of the Titanic, 1912

R.101: the Airship Disaster, 1930

Rillington Place

The Russian Revolution, 1917

The Siege of Kars, 1855

The Siege of the Peking Embassy, 1900

The Strange Story of Adolf Beck

Tragedy at Bethnal Green

Travels in Mongolia, 1902

UFOs in the House of Lords, 1979

War 1914: Punishing the Serbs

War 1939: Dealing with Adolf Hitler

Wilfrid Blunt's Egyptian Garden: Fox-hunting in Cairo

uncovered editions

THE IRISH UPRISING, 1914–21

PAPERS FROM THE BRITISH
PARLIAMENTARY ARCHIVE

∞∞◦◦○◦∞∞

London: The Stationery Office

Applications for reproduction should be made in writing to
The Stationery Office Limited, St Crispins, Duke Street,
Norwich NR3 1PD.

ISBN 0 11 702415 5

First published as Cd 7631, 1914; Cmd 1108, 1921; Cd 8279,
1916; Cd 8376, 1916; Cmd 1470, 1471, 1921.
© Crown copyright

A CIP catalogue record for this book is available from the
British Library.

Cover photograph © Popperfoto: a British officer and two pri-
vates at the scene of some of the worst destruction in Dublin
during the Easter Rebellion of 1916.

Typeset by J&L Composition Ltd, Filey, North Yorkshire.

Printed in the United Kingdom for The Stationery Office by
Biddles Ltd, Guildford, Surrey.

Series editor: Tim Coates

Tim Coates studied at University College, Oxford and at the University of Stirling. After working in the theatre for a number of years, he took up bookselling and became managing director, firstly of Sherratt and Hughes bookshops, and then of Waterstone's. He is known for his support for foreign literature, particularly from the Czech Republic. The idea for 'Uncovered Editions' came while searching through the bookshelves of his late father-in-law, Air Commodore Patrick Cave OBE. He is married to Bridget Cave, has two sons, and lives in London.

Tim Coates welcomes views and ideas on the Uncovered Editions series. He can be e-mailed at timcoatesbooks@yahoo.com

The convention of this series is to add as little as possible to the texts of documents originally published for the British Parliament. The papers are often quite stark, as if the original editor believed that amplification would diminish the impact of what had been written at the time of the events.

Moreover, up to and during the Great War it was the practice to publish information and description that would surprise us today in its openness.

Each of the five documents that are included in this book, is, in its own way, only a small and quite separate part of the events leading to the partition of Ireland in 1921. The book is not in any way a complete description of those events, nor does it offer any explanation of them. For this the reader must seek other histories and commentaries of which there are many.

It seems particularly important in this book to stress that these five papers were originally published exactly as they are written here (with some minor omissions of technical points of law).

In 1914 it was still the case that the whole of Ireland was part of Great Britain, under the dominion of the King, and Irish constituencies were represented in the British Parliament.

Ireland

PART I

❦

REPORT OF THE ROYAL COMMISSION

ON THE

LANDING OF ARMS AT HOWTH

ON

26TH JULY 1914

This is the text of the report of the Royal Commission held to enquire into the landing of arms at Howth, near Dublin, on 26th July 1914, a few days before war broke out in Europe.

The purchase and shipment of arms from Germany to Ireland had been organised by Sir Roger Casement, a well-known Irish nationalist and British diplomat, and Erskine Childers, author of The Riddle of the Sands (1903), an imaginary story of a German raid on England. Both men, under quite separate circumstances and at different times, were later executed for their subversive activities.

Childers navigated his yacht The Asgard across the North Sea to deliver German arms to the Irish Volunteers and the boys of the Fianna, the youth movement of the Irish Citizen Army, who were waiting for the boat to land.

Childers went on to become a member of the Irish parliament for the Irish political party Sinn Fein in 1921. He opposed the Anglo-Irish Treaty of 1921 that established the Irish Free State and was later court-martialled and shot by the Irish Free State authorities.

Sir Roger Casement's fate will be dealt with in the next section.

On or about 12.30 on the afternoon of Sunday, the 26th July, 1914, a yacht entered the harbour of Howth, about 8½ miles from Dublin, and was met by a body of about 1,000 Irish Volunteers. They took possession of the landing place, and unloaded from the yacht a quantity of arms and ammunition. Each man possessed himself of a rifle. Some other rifles were conveyed away along with some ammunition by motor cars and wagons. A few policemen were in the vicinity. They were prevented by the Volunteers from getting through to the pier head, and in a short time the Volunteers to the number of about 800 proceeded

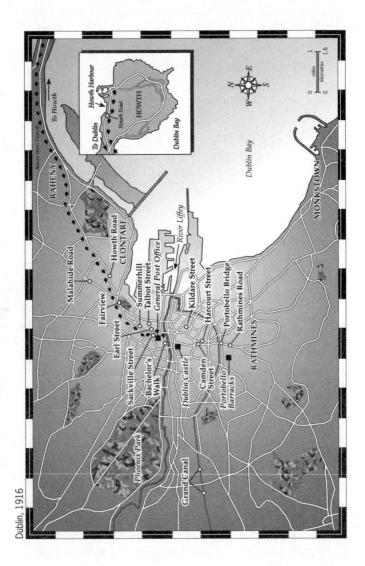

Dublin, 1916

Phoenix Park
Sackville Street
Bachelor's Walk
Earl Street
Fairview
Malahide Road
Summerhill
Talbot Street
General Post Office
Dublin Castle
Camden Street
Kildare Street
Harcourt Street
Portobello Bridge
Rathmines Road
Portobello Barracks
Grand Canal
RATHMINES
CLONTARF
Howth Road
RAHENY
River Liffey
Route from Howth
To Howth
MONKSTOWN
Dublin Bay

Howth Harbour
To Dublin
Howth Road
HOWTH
Dublin Bay

N W E S

miles 0 1
kilometres 0 1.6

to march towards Dublin. The County Inspector of the Royal Irish Constabulary who, with the police, had been at or about the pier, found that his force was unable to prevent the distribution of arms or the landing, both of which in fact had been completed before he could interpose. He, however, communicated by telephone with the "G" Division of the Dublin Metropolitan Police at Exchange Court, an attempt to communicate with Dublin Castle by telephone having failed. In this message he gave information as to what had occurred. The message was dispatched about a few minutes past one. He also states that he endeavoured to get into communication with the Customs Officials and failed.

An Irish Volunteer force had been to the knowledge of the authorities constituted in Dublin some time before these events. It had paraded the streets, and its existence and parades were known to the authorities. It appears to have been composed of respectable citizens, and all of its operations had been conducted without disorder. On the Sunday in question it marched from Howth in good order, and without any interruption, till it reached Raheny, about 3½ miles from Dublin. The Volunteers there halted to rest. They then proceeded as far as the foot of the Howth Road, where they found themselves confronted by a body of police and military, who had assembled at that point. The circumstances under which this had occurred will now be mentioned.

Mr William Vesey Harrel, the Assistant Commissioner of the Dublin Metropolitan Police, at

1.40 p.m. received at his residence in Monkstown, a telephone message to the effect that rifles were being landed at Howth by a body of Irish Volunteers, and that the few police were powerless. Mr Harrel gave telephonic instructions that the Royal Irish Constabulary Depot and the Military Authorities should be informed. He further ordered a force of Dublin Metropolitan Police to proceed by tramway cars to Howth. Shortly afterwards he telephoned to Sir James Dougherty, who was then at his (the Under-Secretary's) Lodge in the Phoenix Park. He informed him of the landing of the rifles, and of the orders sent to the Dublin Metropolitan Police, but he did not inform him of any communication having been made to the military. Sir James Dougherty received this message, and replied that he would at once proceed to the Castle. Mr Harrel is not able to recall this fact, and the telephone seems to have become indistinct. Sir James Dougherty further asked Mr Harrel to communicate with the officers of Coastguards at Kingstown, and he testifies that Mr Harrel said that he had done so. It is the fact that Mr Harrel did wire to the police at Kingstown to let the Coastguards know what had occurred. Up to this stage accordingly what had been done was that a force of Dublin Metropolitan Police had been sent to meet the Volunteers, and that the Military had not been called out.

Mr Harrel went by motor car from his residence to Dublin, and it appears to the Commissioners to be clear that he had from the first resolved to invoke the

aid of the military in the operations which he contemplated. Having ascertained that General Cuthbert,
the Brigadier-General of the Infantry Brigade in
Dublin, was at the Kildare Street Club, he went to
meet him there at about 2.40 p.m. Meanwhile Sir
James Dougherty had arrived by motor car at the
Castle, and as the result of his enquiries for Mr Harrel
he rang up the Kildare Street Club, requesting to
speak to him on the telephone. The message was
delivered to Mr Harrel, who did not comply with the
request. A message, however, by the telephone atten-
dant was given to Sir James Dougherty stating that
Mr Harrel had left the Club. Mr Harrel and General
Cuthbert at once proceeded by motor car to the
Castle. While in his office there at 2.45 a message
from Sir James Dougherty was conveyed to him by
Superintendent Lowe desiring his attendance. This
instruction was not complied with. Mr Harrel says
that he attempted to get into telephonic communication with the Under-Secretary, but that the telephone
was not working. He did not go from his office to the
Under-Secretary's Office, which was about two minutes' walk distant, nor did he take any steps to inform
Sir James Dougherty that he had arrived at the Castle.
His evidence was to the effect that he considered he
had sent the Dublin Police on a somewhat perilous
duty, and that he ought to follow them at once, and
assume responsibility.

As the result of the discussion between Mr Harrel
and General Cuthbert, the latter gave instructions for
the dispatch from Dublin of 100 men of the King's

Own Scottish Borderers, under Captain Cobden, to a point where the Howth Road meets the sea front at Clontarf, and there was subsequently dispatched about sixty men of the same regiment, under Major Coke. Mr Harrel left the Castle after telling Superintendent Lowe "to let Sir James Dougherty know." No information direct or indirect was conveyed to Sir James as to the employment of the Military. Mr Harrel, after a visit to Store Street Police Station, proceeded to Raheny, where he communicated by telephone with General Cuthbert—through the Dublin Police Head Quarters—telling him that the Volunteers were then passing through. Shortly afterwards—about 4 o'clock—Mr Harrel was informed by the Sergeant at Clontarf Police Station that there had been a call for him from the Castle. He did not, however, communicate with the Castle, but proceeded to the foot of Howth Road. It is fairly clear that Mr Harrel up to this point was proceeding upon his own authority, having failed to comply with the request for attendance on the Under-Secretary, or to inform him or any other executive authority that Military were in point of fact being employed.

The result of the measures taken by Mr Harrel and General Cuthbert was that on arrival at the slope which leads down to the foot of Howth Road the Volunteers found their way barred by police and military, drawn up about 150 yards away. The soldiers were the detachment of 100 above mentioned. The Volunteers wheeled to the right, and proceeded by a cross road to the Malahide Road. Mr Harrel, who was then on the spot, decided to head off the Volunteers. A force of fifty Scottish Borderers was accordingly drawn up across the Malahide Road, with a body of about seventy policemen some distance in front of them. Mr Harrel then stepped in front and some discussion took place between him and one or two of the leaders of the Volunteers. This was followed by an order by Mr Harrel to disarm the Volunteers. About nineteen rifles were seized by the police, and also a number of wooden clubs or batons which the Volunteers were carrying. The soldiers took an active part while the struggle was going on, and in the disarmament some bayonet wounds were inflicted upon the Volunteers by them. The Volunteers on their part used clubbed rifles. Meanwhile, those of them in the rear dispersed, and in a few moments the road in front of the police and troops was practically clear. Shortly afterwards about two revolver shots were fired, not by the Volunteers, but by some bystanders unknown, and two of the soldiers received injuries.

Mr Harrel, before leaving Malahide Road, met Sir Neville Chamberlain, the Inspector-General of the Royal Irish Constabulary, and was informed that a force of eighty armed Royal Irish Constabulary were at Amiens Street Station, Dublin. Mr Harrel, however, was satisfied that the affair was over, and very properly said that these men were not required. The detachment of 100 Scottish Borderers, under Captain Cobden, afterwards set off to return to their Barracks in Dublin, and near Fairview about two miles from the city, they were joined by the sixty

Scottish Borderers already mentioned, and under the command of Major Coke. The police were not in company with the troops during the march back to Dublin. They proceeded by a different route. We do not blame anyone for this, but it was, as it turned out, unfortunate. For the presence of a small force of police in the rear of the troops would, in our opinion, have prevented the development of the subsequent fracas between them and the crowd, and they could have at any time dispersed it with ease. Before leaving this part of the narrative we note that Captain Cobden, when actually on the spot, and seeing what was the exact nature of the duties in which the Military were asked to assist, was clearly of opinion that it would have been inadvisable to order his troops to fire upon the Volunteers. His opinion was that the seizure of the contraband rifles would not have justified the taking of life or the inflicting of serious injury upon the Volunteers.

The Clontarf portion of the narrative thus closes.

∞⋄⊗⋄∞

Before making any observation upon the situation or responsibility of parties with regard to it, we deem it advisable to complete the narrative. It may be taken as correct that practically from the time of leaving Clontarf until they passed into the streets of Dublin, and throughout those streets—particularly in Talbot Street, Earl Street and Sackville Street—the soldiers were followed by a crowd, not of very large dimensions, but of insulting demeanour, language, and behaviour. There was some throwing of stones and other missiles. In Dublin itself the news of the intervention of the Military had probably been accompanied with exaggeration and falsehood, and the feeling of many persons became inflamed against the troops. This continued along Bachelor's Walk, into which they had turned from Sackville Street at O'Connell Bridge. By this time Major Haig, who had heard of the disturbances, had joined the force, and being Senior Officer took command. The crowd was occasionally kept in check by the action of the rear guard turning and making feints with fixed bayonets; upon which occasions the crowd dispersed, gathering again in a little time, and still continuing its course of unjustifiable and mischievous misconduct. Upon the other hand the Commissioners do not doubt that the soldiers through great provocation got out of temper and partly out of hand. Sometimes they would pursue the crowd for some distance, chase people into shops, and in one case a soldier drove a bayonet through a shop door. We do not think that the officers could have failed to observe this. We commend the action of Major Coke who by way of precaution repeatedly changed the rear guard by bringing back men from the front whose temper had not been roused. A particularly unfortunate incident was that Major Haig—from his arrival and until the firing upon the crowd by a large body of men—was not aware that the rifles of 100 of these men were loaded.

At about the corner of Liffey Street that officer, being of opinion that the conduct of the crowd was past endurance, told off about thirty men, who turned and lined across the road with fixed bayonets, four or five men kneeling. To five or six of the men Major

Haig spoke hurriedly, asking each if he were loaded, and to be ready to fire if he gave the order. We are not satisfied upon the evidence that there was any particular excess of violence by the crowd at this point although the throwing of stones and other missiles was continuing. A landaulette [small carriage] passed quietly through troops and crowd without any injury. Some witnesses say there was no more than the throwing of banana skins, others that the stone-throwing was severe. We think it proved that one soldier in a tussle with civilians was knocked down. Upon the whole our opinion was that the fracas was just of such a kind as a small force of police would have quickly settled. We are of the opinion that no occasion had actually arisen for using loaded firearms. These were the circumstances in which Major Haig lined up his men, and instructed them as mentioned.

That officer stated in evidence that, first, his intention was to warn the crowd, and, secondly, in the event of the threatening and stone-throwing by the crowd continuing, he would have asked that those men so spoken to should shoot two particular ring-leaders to be pointed out by himself. He plainly disapproved in his evidence of the action and notion of an order given to troops in general to fire indiscriminately upon a crowd. This, however, was what occurred. We are satisfied that neither Major Haig, nor any of his fellow officers, did give an order to fire. But not only did firing take place without an order, but it was indiscriminate firing. Twenty-one men discharged their rifles at the crowd. Twenty-nine shots were fired. Three people were killed; at least thirty-eight people were injured, and fifteen of these so seriously as to be detained in hospital. It is a feature also of the transaction that one of the dead and some of the injured appeared to have had upon their bodies not only bullet but bayonet wounds.

The dead were: Mrs Mary Duffy, aged 50; Patrick Quinn, aged 46; and James Brennan, aged 18.

The firing, in short, was at large, without distinction of age or sex, and was at short range. We are glad to think that the fatal results were so few.

With regard to Major Haig's position, his object of addressing the crowd was not attained. He went in front of his men, and raised his hand; and this act appears to have been misinterpreted by at least one of the soldiers as equivalent to an order to fire. Some of the soldiers think that they heard an order although not from Major Haig. Others concluded that there must have been an order when one shot was fired, and so they also fired. The men, in our opinion, showed a lack of self-control and of discipline, and we cannot but think that their excitement and annoyance under the provocation they were subjected to, may have been productive in their minds of the misapprehension as to an order having been given. As it was, Major Haig's lifting of his hand was followed not by the discharge of the rifles of the men whom he had selected, but by the discharge of the rifles of twenty-one men, with regard to at least sixteen of whom he was unaware of the fact that they were in possession of loaded weapons.

Before leaving the narrative of events it may be desirable for us to deal with the action of two high State officials in Ireland whose conduct with reference thereto has, we understand, been subjected to some adverse criticism. These are Sir James Dougherty, Under-Secretary for Ireland, and the Lord Chancellor of Ireland.

On the day in question, the Chief Secretary being absent from Ireland, the Under-Secretary, subject to the orders of the Lord Lieutenant, was the chief Executive Officer in the country, and was the person to whom naturally an appeal would be made upon the question of a demand by the civil power for the intervention of the military authorities. Sir James was in residence at the Under-Secretary's Lodge, about three miles from Dublin Castle. About 2 o'clock he received the telephone message from Mr Harrel, already mentioned. In answer he instructed Mr Harrel to communicate with the Deputy Inspector-General (Mr O'Connell), and with the officers of Coastguards at Kingstown, and he was informed that this had already been done. He said that he would at once go down to the Castle, but this message Mr Harrel does not recollect receiving, and as mentioned the telephone became indistinct. No question or suggestion was made about military intervention. Sir James drove by motor car, without any avoidable delay to the Castle, sent for the Deputy-Inspector-General of the Royal Irish Constabulary (Mr O'Connell), and for Mr Harrel. Mr O'Connell at once attended, but Mr Harrel did not. Mr O'Connell explained that he had been informed that the body of Volunteers had by that time—say, 2.35—already left Howth, being in possession of their rifles, and were on their way to Dublin. It at once occurred to Sir James that "a legal question would arise under the altered circumstances," and he set about procuring the highest available legal advice.

Neither the Attorney-General nor Solicitor-General were in the City, or could be communicated with. It occurred to him, however, to consult the Lord Chancellor of Ireland, and that learned judge after giving through the telephone his views, which were adverse to any attempt to seize arms, or to interfere with the men on the march to Dublin, was good enough to proceed personally from his residence at Dundrum by motor car to the Castle, where he arrived at 3.15. Both officials, being anxious in mind, and Mr Harrel not having arrived, they themselves proceeded at about four o'clock to the Dublin Metropolitan Police Office, where they were informed by Sir John Ross that there was information that two soldiers had been shot. This was the first intimation that either of them had had that soldiers had ever been employed. They could get no definite information as to where Mr Harrel was to be found. Thereupon they at once returned, and framed a minute in the following terms:

> As regards the steps which you have taken on your own responsibility to deal with the arms landed at Howth this morning, His Excellency is advised that forcible disarmament of the men now marching into Dublin with these arms should not be attempted; but the names of the men carrying the arms should be taken, and watch should be kept to ascertain the destination of the arms illegally imported.

This Sir James addressed to the Assistant Commissioner. It was sent at once to his office, opened by Sir John Ross the Chief Commissioner, and is understood to have been dispatched by him by messenger on a bicycle to Mr Harrel. Mr Harrel says it was delivered to him at Amiens Street Railway

Station at about 5.45. The various efforts made by Sir James Dougherty to obtain the attendance of and an interview with Mr Harrel have been already detailed. They all failed. We feel bound to put upon record our opinion that throughout these events we cannot find that the conduct of Sir James Dougherty was in any respect blameworthy. On the contrary we regret that his opinion was not obtained and acted upon. Had it been, then in our judgment the illegalities and casualties of the afternoon would have been avoided.

Recognising as we do the delicacy of some of the legal problems which the events raised, we commend the desire of the Under-Secretary for the guidance of the Law Officers, and the prompt and ready response made in their absence by the Lord Chancellor of Ireland. His Lordship completely confirms the Under-Secretary as to the information that the military had been called out having been obtained for the first time as stated, and as to the minute having been promptly framed and forwarded to Mr Harrel. The suggestion that this minute had its origin in any desire to save any Castle official from responsibility, or had any *arrière pensée* of a sinister character, appears to us to be quite groundless. As to the contents of the minute itself there seems much in good sense to recommend the course which it prescribed. We say this, apart from the questions of illegality to which we shall afterwards refer.

In closing this part of the narrative it appears to us that we ought to say that the evidence discloses no case of chronic irritation, but upon the contrary indicates the prevalence of cordial good feeling between the population of Dublin and the soldiers quartered in that city. We note the action and practice of the Under-Secretary and the other Authorities as thus expressed by Sir James Dougherty in a passage of his evidence to which we desire to direct attention:

> My opinion on the subject of calling out the military to aid the police in street rows is pretty well known, I think. We have had a good many labour disputes in the City of Dublin, and I have incurred some odium because I set my face against employing the military unless the case was one of overwhelming necessity. In taking that position I had the sympathy and support of high military authorities—the present Commander-in-Chief of the Forces in Ireland, and his predecessor, General Lyttleton.

On this head of the Inquiry we record our view that the policy thus described by the Under-Secretary not only appears to be commendable and proper, but to be also in our opinion, in accordance with sound law. And we venture to express the hope that after the irritation caused by the events under review has subsided, the relations of good feeling and good-will between the population and the military in the City of Dublin may be resumed.

We shall now proceed to apply the code of law and practice to the events which are the subject of this Enquiry.

Sir James Dougherty, Under-Secretary for Ireland, stands free from blame.

With regard to Mr Harrel, while we do not discount his evidence that he had in his mind the notion that the Irish Volunteers on their march constituted an unlawful assembly, which it was legitimate to attempt to disperse by force, we think that his real and true object was the seizure of the contraband rifles. We unhesitatingly accept the evidence of General Cuthbert that "he (Mr Harrel) considered it to be his duty to try and take these arms, and to do so he asked me for the assistance of the military." We are of the opinion that the calling in even of the police for this, which was a Customs duty, was not warranted by law. Due employment for the prevention of smuggling would have been required under the Customs Act. There was no such employment; and Your Majesty's Proclamation could not give, and did not purport to give, any greater power than that contained in the Statute. The whole transaction was then, illegal from beginning to end, and the orders of Mr Harrel were *ultra vires*, and his action of seizure of rifles was not in the due execution of the law.

If this be so with regard to the police it is of course *a fortiori* so in regard to the calling in of the military. They were called in to support an illegality by force of arms. So much on the head of the seizure of the rifles, so far as Mr Harrel is concerned. We shall deal separately with the conduct of General Cuthbert on this head.

We are of further opinion that the Volunteers on the road to Dublin were not an assembly which it was either judicious or legal to treat as demanding the employment of the military. The possession of rifles imported as described may possibly have laid the Volunteers open to suitable proceedings taken under the Customs Acts. But their assembly was not characterised by violence, crime, riot, disturbance, or the likelihood of any of these things. The law or the King's Regulations could not be invoked, on the principles already explained, in defence of calling in military assistance, for which in our view neither the occasion nor the circumstances furnished justification. We feel bound to add moreover that the principle of falling back on military aid as a last resort was completely ignored. To call in the soldiers was among the first things thought of. Further, the serious consequences of the employment of the military upon such an errand do not appear to have occurred to or at least impressed Mr Harrel's mind. In short, the position and attitude of the Assistant Commissioner—which we do not further analyse—we find it difficult to follow, in view of his local knowledge and long experience. We cannot but conclude, however, that the neglect of those principles and rules of practice which should have been followed was one of the causes of the unfortunate events which ensued.

With regret we have to make the same observation with regard to General Cuthbert. We appreciate the position of a military officer called upon suddenly by the civil power to give aid in regard to civil commotion. The civil authority presumably knows, and the officer away from the scene does not know, whether the circumstances warrant troops being called out. This being so, the officer may in most situations accept the word of the magistrate or civil functionary in the initial act of ordering his men out. But the present was not a case of that kind. To begin with, General Cuthbert had no written requisition. Had he had it might have given him pause. Presumably it would have contained a precise intimation of the exact object and a statement that the police had been prevented by combined force or were likely to be so prevented from achieving this object. But General Cuthbert clearly understood what it was that his troops were to be sent out to do. He does not appear to have considered whether it was a case to which the ordinary and familiar principles as to military intervention applied; in fact he knew it was not. As to the order itself, viz., to seize rifles, he would have been well warranted in the absence of any demand by the Customs authorities in refusing to comply with any such requisition. To refuse it was, in our opinion, his duty. We regret that he did not fully consider the position, which on consideration we feel sure that he would have seen in its true light, viz., that an attempt was being made to put soldiers to a duty which the law did not impose, and would not warrant.

We do not doubt, however, that this action provoked in the minds of the population the idea that some discrimination relatively unfavourable to its independence and freedom was being made against the City of Dublin. This was the case. But it was the case not by reason of the Government or of the law, but by individual action taken without the sanction of either. And we may note one singular illustration of how quickly the view of indiscriminate or uneven administration is apprehended and resented. When the order to seize rifles was given, eighteen of the police, whose obedience and discipline are notorious, refused to obey, one of their number who was examined before us gave their reason, viz., that the disarming could surely not be legal as it had not been done in Belfast. The eighteen were at once withdrawn from action, and two of them, including the witness referred to, were dismissed on the following evening. We only cite the incident to illustrate how disastrous to contentment and to order it would be if the law were partially or unevenly administered.

GENERAL CONCLUSIONS

It may be now convenient that we should state in the form of a brief compend, the general conclusions at which we have arrived. They are as follows:

(1) The employment of the police and the military was not in accordance with law, and in particular was not in compliance with section 202 of the Customs Act of 1876.

(2) Mr Harrel, Assistant Commissioner of Police, is responsible for calling out the military, as well as

for the orders issued to the Dublin Metropolitan
Police.

(3) We cannot hold that Sir James Dougherty,
Under-Secretary for Ireland, failed in any
respect in his duty to the Crown or to the
public. As already stated, he stands free of blame.

(4) General Cuthbert should have considered
whether the task which his troops were called
on to perform, viz., the seizure of arms, was
invoked by proper authority, and was in itself a
proper one to discharge under the King's
regulations, and the law. He did not adequately
consider these things, and his compliance with
the Assistant Commissioner's call was wrong.

(5) There was no compliance with the specific rule
requiring a written requisition.

(6) This is regrettable, because we incline to the
opinion that the written order might have
induced General Cuthbert more scrupulously to
consider the nature of the proposed duty.

(7) In our view—and apart from the fundamental
illegality as to the seizure of rifles—there was in
the events and circumstances set forth no case
warranting military intervention.

(8) Apart from the question of the possession of
contraband rifles, with which we have already
dealt, the gathering of the Irish Volunteers, and
their march towards Dublin, did not constitute
an unlawful assembly requiring dispersal by
military aid. Their presence or conduct
produced no terror to the lieges, and did not in

our opinion endanger life or property or the King's peace. The calling in of the military to quell or suppress this gathering as an unlawful assembly was, in our opinion, unjustifiable.

(9) At the scene of conflict near Clontarf the conduct of Mr Harrel in parleying with the leaders of the crowd, and of Captain Cobden in resolving against firing was prudent and correct.

(10) Between Fairview and Bachelor's Walk the military were subjected to insults and assailed with missiles, but, in our opinion, there was no such great and inevitable danger of serious bodily harm as to justify the use of firearms.

(11) In Bachelor's Walk the command by Major Haig to five or six men to prepare to fire under his order we do not pronounce upon. For we hold it not proved that an actual order to fire was given *or* that any order to fire proceeded from any officers. It is manifest that any general or promiscuous order would have been improper. This Major Haig recognised at the time, and we are satisfied that such an order, viz., for promiscuous firing, would not have been given by him.

(12) In the circumstances which we have set forth it is regrettable that Major Haig was not informed when he joined the forces in Dublin that the rifles were loaded.

(13) The promiscuous firing of rifles by twenty-one soldiers took place without orders; but we

think that the troops were under the
impression that the order was given either
directly or passed from man to man.

In regard to these conclusions we beg to report that
they are unanimous. The report is also in all particulars a unanimous report.

We humbly trust that we may be excused for
mentioning another point. We are convinced that
many of the victims who suffered by the firing in
Bachelor's Walk were innocent of all connection with
the unseemly outrageous and provocative action of
the crowd, but were passive spectators or ordinary
pedestrians. In these cases and indeed in all, the results
to those injured and especially to the relatives of those
who were shot dead are such as to evoke both deep
regret and unfeigned compassion. It is not properly in
our province to do more than to commend all these
cases to the sympathetic consideration of the Lords of
the Treasury.

SHAW OF DUNFERMLINE
WILLIAM D. ANDREWS
T. F. MOLONY

ALEXANDER SHAW, *Secretary*
4th September, 1914

PART II

∞∞⬦∞∞

DOCUMENTS
RELATIVE TO THE
SINN FEIN MOVEMENT

1921

The following documents were published in 1921 by the British Government, as evidence of the collusion between Germany and Sinn Fein prior to the Easter Rising of 1916.

These documents reveal how Sir Roger Casement negotiated a further shipment of German arms, the arrival of which was intended to coincide with and provide weapons for the planned uprising throughout Ireland in April 1916.

The British Government, now in the midst of the Great War, gathered information on this activity, intercepted the landing, and arrested Sir Roger Casement at Tralee in County Kerry. Casement was later executed for high treason, on the instruction of the Cabinet in London, in August 1916.

In May 1918 His Majesty's Government published a statement which, so far as was then expedient in the public interest, summarised without disclosing sources of information and channels of communication, evidence and documents in the possession of the Government showing the active connection between the leaders of the Sinn Fein Movement and the German Government.

The following statement reveals (so far as seems at present expedient) in detail certain of the documents proving the intrigues between Sinn Fein and Germany.

It is desirable for the purpose of throwing light upon some of these documents to mention certain facts which occurred before war was declared in August 1914.

In 1911, 1912, 1913 and 1914 a series of articles appeared in seditious Irish newspapers and in various organs of the Irish American press in the United States urging a German Irish Alliance in the event of war between Germany and England, and they were widely circulated also in pamphlet form. One of them was *Ireland, Germany and the next War.* It was re-issued immediately on the outbreak of the war together with another entitled *The Crime against Europe*. Sir Roger Casement was the author of these two pamphlets. This literature insisted on the strategic importance of Ireland as a factor of supreme importance in relation to sea power, and urged that in the event of England being defeated Ireland would at the Peace Conference secure through Germany her independence.

In 1912 the first-mentioned of Casement's articles was sent by him to Von Bernhardi. It was translated and widely circulated in Germany and attracted considerable attention and discussion in the German press. Immediately after war was declared Kuno Meyer, who had been Professor of Celtic Languages in Liverpool University, became associated with Casement in reproducing these and similar articles in a cheap pamphlet form grouped together under the title:

IRELAND, GERMANY AND THE FREEDOM OF THE SEAS.
A POSSIBLE OUTCOME OF THE WAR OF 1914.
TO FREE THE SEAS, FREE IRELAND.

Large quantities of the pamphlet were printed in Germany as well as in America. Excerpts were also issued in leaflet form and immense numbers were smuggled into Ireland and circulated as German propaganda by Sinn Fein.

The introduction to the pamphlet prepared by Casement and Kuno Meyer explains the character of this propaganda which had been commenced in 1911:

> The following articles were begun in 1911 under the title, *Ireland, Germany and the Next War*, and were intended for private circulation only among a few interested friends of both countries.
>
> Part I was written in August 1911, Parts II to IV were written at odd moments, between the end of 1912 and November 1913.
>
> The whole six parts furnish in outline the case for a German–Irish alliance as this presented itself to the writer's mind when the world was still at peace.
>
> It was the writer's intention to show in succeeding chapters how the vital needs of European peace, of European freedom of the seas and of Irish national life and prosperity were indissolubly linked with the cause of Germany in the struggle so clearly impending between that country and Great Britain.
>
> The war has come sooner than was expected.
> The rest of the writer's task must be essayed not with

the author's pen, but with the rifle of the Irish
Volunteer. As a contribution to the cause of Irish
freedom this presentment of the cause for Germany,
friend of Ireland and foe of England, is now
published.

When the war began Casement was in America.
He was in close touch with the Irish Revolutionary
Associations there. John Devoy, the ex-Fenian, was
the most prominent leader of these Associations. He
was during the war the chief agent in America for
communication between Germany and Sinn Fein,
and was described by Von Skal, one of Count Von
Bernstorff's staff in Washington, as their "Confidential
Agent" in a despatch from the German Embassy in
America to Berlin in February 1916. He was known
as "Sean Fear" (The Old Man) among the Irish revolutionaries. Casement left America and arrived in
Germany shortly after the war had commenced, and
(as will appear from the documents disclosed) he
maintained communication with Devoy through the
Germans. He had also been suggesting to the German
Embassy the formation of an Irish Legion from Irish
prisoners of war. The Germans arranged for
Casement's return to Berlin where he had been prior
to his visit to America.

*The following despatches were exchanged between the German
Embassy in America and the Foreign Office in Berlin.*

German Embassy, Washington, to Foreign Office, Berlin
27th September, 1914

I am telegraphing, because written reports are too unsafe. I do not think it necessary in this matter to be too much exercised about American public opinion, as we are most likely to find friends here if we give freedom to oppressed peoples, such as the Poles, the Finns and the Irish. What American public opinion is afraid of, so far as it is against us, is in the event of our victory, an excessive extension of our frontiers over areas where foreign languages are spoken. The decisive point seems to me to lie in the question whether any prospect of an understanding with England is now in view, or must we prepare ourselves for a life and death struggle? If so, I recommend falling in with Irish wishes, provided that there are really Irishmen who are prepared to help. The form-ation of an Irish Legion from Irish prisoners of war would be a grand idea if only it could be carried out.

It is said that the Irish Catholic priest Sexton, teacher at the Stilly Institute in Berlin, and nephew of the Bishop of Cork, is being detained in Berlin. The Irish here request that his return to Ireland may be facilitated. Irishmen here declare that Catholic Ireland will provide no voluntary recruits for England.

German Embassy, Washington, to Foreign Office, Berlin
1st October, 1914

An Irish priest [*sic*] named Michael Collins and Sir Roger Casement are going to Germany in order to visit the Irish prisoners. I have given the former a recommendation to F.

Casement has received a cable from Dublin reporting that the whole of the twenty-five members nominated by Redmond on the Committee of the Irish Volunteers have been expelled from the Committee on account of Redmond's attempt to induce the Irish Volunteers to enter the English army.

Foreign Office, Berlin, to German Embassy, Washington
3rd November, 1914

Sir Roger Casement has arrived. His proposals are being carefully gone into.

ZIMMERMAN

Zimmermann was the Secretary of State for Foreign Affairs at Berlin.

Foreign Office, Berlin, to German Embassy, Washington
6th November, 1914

Casement begs that the following intelligence may be transmitted:

"For Justice Cohalan, 51, Chambers Street, New York.

"Lody's identity discovered by enemy who are greatly alarmed and taking steps to defend Ireland and possibly arrest friends. They are ignorant here of the purpose of my coming to Germany, but seek evidence at all cost. Here everything favourable: authority helping warmly.

Send messenger immediately to Ireland fully
informed verbally. No letter upon him. He
should be native-born American citizen,
otherwise arrest likely. Let him despatch priest
here via Christiania [Oslo] quickly. German
Legation there will arrange passage; also let him
tell Bigger, solicitor, Belfast to conceal everything
belonging to me.   ROGER"

ZIMMERMAN

Lody mentioned in the despatch was a German spy
who was arrested at Killarney on the 2nd October,
1914, and executed in the Tower on the 6th
November, 1914. On the 20th November, 1914, the
following official statement was issued from the
German Foreign Office. It was circulated to the
German press and sent out by wireless telegram. It
was printed as a leaflet in Berlin and America and sent
in great quantities to Sinn Fein and German agents in
Ireland, where it was distributed extensively:

GERMANY AND IRELAND

Berlin, November 20th, 1914

The well-known Irish Nationalist, Sir Roger
Casement, who has arrived in Berlin from the United
States, has been received at the Foreign Office. Sir
Roger Casement pointed out that statements were
being published in Ireland, apparently with the
authority of the British Government behind them, to
the effect that a German victory would inflict great

loss upon the Irish people, whose homes, churches, priests and lands would be at the mercy of an invading army actuated only by motives of pillage and conquest. Recent utterances of Mr Redmond on his recruiting tour in Ireland and many pronouncements of the British press in Ireland to the above effect have been widely circulated, Sir Roger pointed out, and have caused natural apprehension among Irishmen as to the German attitude towards Ireland in the event of a German victory in the present war.

Sir Roger sought a convincing statement of German intentions towards Ireland that might reassure his countrymen all over the world, and particularly in Ireland and America, in view of these disquieting statements emanating from responsible British quarters.

In reply to this enquiry, the Acting Secretary of State at the Foreign Office, by order of the Imperial Chancellor, has made the following official declaration:

Official Statement

The German Government repudiates the evil intentions attributed to it in the statements referred to by Sir Roger Casement, and takes this opportunity to give a categoric assurance that the German Government desires only the welfare of the Irish people, their country, and their institutions.

The Imperial Government formally declares that under no circumstances would Germany invade

Ireland with a view to its conquest or the overthrow of any native institutions in that country.

Should the fortune of this great war, that was not of Germany's seeking, ever bring in its course German troops to the shores of Ireland, they would land there, not as an army of invaders to pillage and destroy, but as the forces of a Government that is inspired by good-will towards a country and a people for whom Germany desires only NATIONAL PROSPERITY and NATIONAL FREEDOM.

The following letters which were intercepted were written by Casement and enclosed in a covering envelope addressed to a lady then in London. The letter to Professor Eoin McNeill requests him to have the official declaration of the German Government published throughout Ireland by every possible means.

LETTER

Send this on by hand. Read it if you like: it is a sacred confidence. But send it on by sure means.

With much love and affection from the Man of Three Cows. He is well, and has convincing assurance of help, recognition, friends, and comfort for the poor old woman. All that he asks for will be given her and the stranger put out of her house for ever. He has seen the big men, and they are one with his views, and if successful they will aid to uttermost to redeem the four green fields.

SECOND ENVELOPE

Not to go through post on any account.

Professor Eoin McNeill,

19, Herbert Park

Ball's Bridge

Dublin

Berlin, 28th November, 1914

Please have this official declaration of the German Government, stating its intentions and declaring the goodwill of the German people towards Ireland and the desire of both Government and people for Irish national freedom published throughout Ireland by every possible means.

You know who writes this. I am in Berlin, and if Ireland will do her duty, rest assured Germany will do hers towards us, our cause, and our whole future.

The enemy are doing everything to keep the truth out of Ireland, and are even going to try to get the Vatican on their side, as in the time of Parnell. Once our people, clergy and volunteers know that Germany, if victorious, will do her best to aid us in our efforts to achieve an independent Ireland, every man at home must stand for Germany and Irish freedom.

I am entirely assured of the goodwill of this Government towards our country, and beg you to proclaim it far and wide. They will do all in their power to help us to win national freedom, and it lies with Ireland and Irishmen themselves to prove that they are worthy to be free.

Send to me here in Berlin, by way of Christiania [Oslo], if possible, one or two thoroughly patriotic

Irish priests—young men best. Men like Father Murphy of Vinegar Hill—*and for the same purpose.*

Rifles and ammunition can be found and good officers, too. First send the priest or priests, as I need them for a special purpose here, you can guess— for—

If the priest or priests can get to Christiania (Norway), they can get here through the German Legation at Christiania. Our friends in America will pay all expenses. Warn all our people, too, of the present intrigue at Rome to bring pressure of religion to bear on a question wholly political and national. Our enemy will stick at no crime to-day against Ireland, as you will soon know. This official declaration of the German Government has been sent out to all the German representatives abroad for world-wide publication. It may be followed by another still more to the point—but much depends on your staunchness and courage at home.

Tell all to trust the Germans—and to trust me. We shall win everything if you are brave and faithful to the old cause. Try and send me word here to Berlin by the same channel as this. Tell me all your needs at home, viz., rifles, officers, men. Send priest or priests at all costs—one not afraid to *fight* and die for Ireland. The enemy are hiding the truth. The Germans will surely, under God, defeat both Russia and France and compel a peace that will leave Germany stronger than before. They already have 550,000 prisoners of war in Germany, and Austria

150,000, and Russia has been severely defeated in Poland.

India and Egypt will probably both be in arms. Even if Germany cannot reach England to-day, we can only gain by helping Germany now, as with the understanding come to, Ireland will have a strong and enlightened friend to help to ultimate independence.

We may win everything by this war if we are true to Germany; and if we do not win to-day we ensure international recognition of Irish nationality and hand on an uplifted cause for our sons.

Reply by this route: a letter for me, addressed to Mr Hammond, 76, Wilhelmstrasse, Berlin, to be enclosed in one addressed to Messrs. Wambersin and Son, Rotterdam.

With regard to Casement's statement that India would probably be in arms, it appears that in October 1914 Chempakaraman Pillai, who will be found afterwards associated with the German-Irish Society, was employed by the German Foreign Office in Berlin and established there the Indian National Party attached to the German General Staff. The members of this "staff" were engaged in the production of anti-British literature for propaganda; in directing a campaign to win Indian prisoners of war captured by the Germans from the British ranks from their allegiance; and in arranging for the smuggling of arms into India. A Captain Boehm (whose name will appear further down) was engaged in making arrangements in the United States with Indian agents

of Germany in America to despatch cargoes of arms
and ammunition to the Indian revolutionaries. Arms
were shipped, but captured. The methods and fate of
these Indian intrigues were very similar to those of
the German dealings with Sinn Fein.

German Embassy, Washington, to Foreign Office, Berlin
December 1914

For Casement:

Confidential agent arrived in Ireland at end of
November.

The declaration of the German Foreign Office
has made an excellent impression.

The priest starts as soon as the leave of absence
which he requires has been granted. This is expected
soon.

Judge Cohalan recommends not publishing
statement about attempt on Casement's life until
actual proofs are secured.

Requests for money have been complied with.

There have been purchased for India, eleven
thousand rifles, four million cartridges, two hundred
and fifty Mauser pistols, five hundred revolvers with
ammunition. Devoy does not think it possible to ship
them to Ireland.

I am trying to buy rifles for Turkey in South
America.

German Embassy, Washington, to Foreign Office, Berlin
13th December, 1914

Please remit a thousand dollars to Sir Roger
Casement, which have been paid to me by Mr
Devoy, of the Gaelic American.

For Casement:

O'Donnel cannot go.

Reverend John T. Nicholson, of Philadelphia, is
on sick leave now and ready to start.

First available vessel sails for Netherlands
December 18th. Arranged to have pass for Italy and
Switzerland.

Is in every way qualified. Speaks Irish well. Has
visited Germany and is in full sympathy with the
work we want done. Born in Ireland, but is American
citizen.

Foreign Office, Berlin, to German Embassy, Washington
EXTRACT FROM MESSAGE
28th January, 1915

Please pass on the two following instructions as
promptly as possible:

1st. To John Devoy:

Support of Larkin entails loss of sympathy in
many quarters of Ireland. Send all possible literature
to Collegio Irlandese, Rome.

2nd. To J. M'Garrity, Philadelphia:

Send by Ambassador's Messenger at once a copy
of *The Crime against Europe* to Hammond. I can
publish here.

The Crime against Europe was (as above stated) incorporated with other of Casement's articles in the pamphlet *Ireland, Germany and the Freedom of the Seas. A Possible Outcome of the War of 1914. To Free the Seas, Free Ireland.* The pamphlet was printed and published both in Germany and in America.

Casement after his arrival in Germany was actively engaged in endeavouring to seduce Irish prisoners of war from their allegiance. An attempt which was almost a complete failure. Kuno Meyer was associated with him in this scheme.

A letter was written from the Berlin Foreign Office on 28th December, 1914, addressed to Casement by the Under-Secretary of State for Foreign Affairs, Herr Zimmermann. It stated that the Imperial Government had accepted Casement's proposal for the formation of an Irish Brigade to fight only in the cause of Irish nationality under the conditions contained in the contract already concluded between Casement and the German Government. These conditions provided that in certain circumstances the Irish Brigade should be sent to Ireland well furnished with stores and munitions to help to equip the Irish for a united attempt to restore freedom to Ireland by force of arms. Among the special conditions mentioned were the following, namely, that in the event of a German naval victory rendering it possible to reach Ireland, the German Government undertook to assist the Irish Brigade with a German auxiliary corps under the command of German officers in German transports which would be landed on

the Irish coast. The landing in Ireland would, however, only be considered expedient in the event of a
German victory offering good prospects for a successful passage to Ireland, failing which, the Irish
Brigade would be employed in Germany or elsewhere, solely, however, in the manner already agreed
upon with Casement. In such a contingency the Irish
Brigade might be sent to Egypt to render assistance in
restoring Egyptian independence.

On the 6th December, 1914, Kuno Meyer
addressed a meeting of the Clan-na-Gael, of Long
Island, New York.

It was in the summer of 1911 (he said) that I lost all
hope of peace between England and Germany. I have
visited many of our prisoners' camps, and had many
talks with the English and Irish among them. At a
station called Lohne I fell in with a train containing
Irish soldiers who were being drafted from all parts of
Germany into one camp for the mysterious purpose
which I have hinted at before. That an invasion both
of England and Ireland will take place sooner or later
I, together with all my countrymen, firmly believe.
The attack upon Yarmouth, the mines placed near
Malin Head, and what happened in Lough Swilly
and at Sheerness have already foreshadowed it. And
when Germany has obtained the great objects for
which she fights, the nations that now bear the yoke
of England unwillingly will, surely, not be forgotten,
and in the case of two of them at least, the oldest and
the youngest of England's conquests, Ireland and

Egypt, the restitution of their autonomy must be one of the conditions of peace. (See *The Times*, 24th December, 1914.)

For an account of the proceedings of Sinn Fein in Ireland and its connection there with the Irish Revolutionary Association in America, in alliance with the German organisations there, down to the outbreak of the Rebellion of Easter 1916, reference is made to the Report of the Royal Commission on the Rebellion in Ireland 1916. The report states:

> It is now a matter of common notoriety that the Irish volunteers have been in communication with the authorities in Germany, and were, for a long time, known to be supplied with money through Irish-American societies. It was so stated in public by Mr John McNeill on 8th November, 1914. It was suspected long before the outbreak that some of the money came from German sources.

Early in 1915 after the promulgation in Ireland of military orders under the Defence of the Realm Act for the action of the inhabitants in the event of invasion, counter notices were placarded calling on the people to disobey the orders issued and to welcome the German troops as friends. The following is a specimen notice:

PEOPLE OF WEXFORD
Take no notice of the police order to destroy your own property, and leave your homes if a German

army lands in Ireland. When the Germans come they will come as friends, and to put an end to English rule in Ireland. Therefore, stay in your homes, and assist as far as possible the German troops. Any stores, hay, corn, or forage taken by the Germans will be paid for by them.

In February 1915 great quantities of this proclamation and of the "Official Statement" in the leaflet *Germany and Ireland*, which had been printed in Berlin, were discovered at Enniscorthy, in the house of Laurence De Lacey, who evaded arrest and fled to America. He was subsequently sentenced to imprisonment at San Francisco for plotting with German agents there. After his escape to America, De Lacey was in touch with the Sinn Fein Party in Ireland.

The Friends of Peace

In February 1915, Albert Sander, a German spy, who had offices at 150, Nassau Street, New York, formed an organisation called the "Friends of Peace", the object of the society being to assist Germany in securing an embargo on the exportation of arms from the United States, and to prevent America from entering the war. Linked up and affiliated with this society were the Clan-na-Gael, the Socialist Party of New York, a German-Irish association called "The American Truth Society," and a number of German-American societies, and among the chairmen were John Devoy and John A. O'Leary.

In February 1917, Sander was convicted in New York for initiating and providing in the United States for a military enterprise against Great Britain and Ireland and sending spies to Great Britain and Ireland, and was sentenced to two years' imprisonment.

The following despatches were sent in January 1916 from Berlin to Washington, and afterwards published by the American Secretary of State:

German Foreign Office to Count Von Bernstorff

3rd January 1916 (*secret*)

General Staff desires energetic action in regard to proposed destruction of Canadian Pacific Railway at several points with a view to complete and protracted interruption of traffic. Capt. Boehm who is known on your side and is shortly returning has been given instructions. Inform the Military Attaché and provide the necessary funds.

ZIMMERMAN

January 26, for Military Attaché.

You can obtain particulars as to persons suitable for carrying on sabotage in the United States and Canada from the following persons:

(1) Joseph M'Garrity, Philadelphia, Pa.; (2) John P. Keating, Michigan Avenue, Chicago; (3) Jeremiah O'Leary, 16, Park Row, New York. One and two are absolutely reliable, but not always discreet. These persons are indicated by Sir Roger Casement. In the United States sabotage can be carried out on every kind of factory for supplying munitions of war.

Railway embankments and bridges must not be touched. Embassy must in no circumstances be compromised. Similar precautions must be taken in regard to Irish pro-German propaganda.

Representative of General Staff

Foreign Office, Berlin, to German Embassy, Washington
5th January, 1916

For John Devoy:

Letter 21st November received; office unnecessary, no further men needed.

Casement

The Friends of Irish Freedom

Shortly before the rebellion of Easter 1916 there was founded in the United States the association known as "The Friends of Irish Freedom".

In February 1916 Judge Cohalan, T. St John Gaffney, and Jeremiah A. O'Leary issued a call for an Irish Race Convention which was held in New York on the 4th and 5th March, 1916. A permanent organisation was then formed. The president, three of the vice-presidents, the treasurer and secretary were members of the Clan-na-Gael; Judge Cohalan was first of the board of directors; Jeremiah O'Leary and Joseph M'Garrity were on the executive. Of the 52 permanent members of the board of directors, 37 were members of the Clan-na-Gael, and of the 17 members of the executive, 15 belonged to the Clan-na-Gael. John Devoy was one of the association and T. St John Gaffney was appointed representative of the Friends of Irish Freedom for Europe. A bureau was established at Stockholm, whither Gaffney repaired, and from there and at Berlin maintained, along with George Chatterton-Hill, close relations between the German Government and the various Irish-American and Sinn Fein organisations. De Valera, Monteith, Mellowes and others of the Irish Sinn Fein rebels who went to America after the Rebellion became participators in the work of the Friends of Irish Freedom.

This congress was convened for the purpose of "arranging means to enable Ireland to recover independence after the war". The convention demanded the recognition of Ireland as an independent nation, and passed a resolution that:

> We hereby appeal to the Great Powers to recognise that Ireland is a European island and not an English island, and to appreciate the fact that the complete independence of Ireland from the Britannic Empire is the essential and indispensable condition of the freedom of the seas.

The Friends of Irish Freedom maintained close touch with the German organisations in America both before and after the rebellion.

The bureau of the Friends of Irish Freedom in Stockholm was at 286 Artillerigatan, and was under the direction of T. St John Gaffney. He will be found acting along with Chatterton-Hill as the accredited agent of Sinn Fein at Stockholm and Berlin in 1917 and 1918.

The Indiska Central Committee (an Indian seditious organisation) shared quarters at 286 Artillerigatan with the Friends of Irish Freedom.

◦◦◦◦◦◦

*Despatch addressed to Mr W. Pfitzner, Esschenlaan 16,
Rotterdam, sent per SS "Sommelsdyk".*

Most Secret   *New York,* 10*th February,* 1916
Extract from report of Confidential Agent, John
Devoy, on the position in Ireland, which has been
delivered to the Imperial Embassy for telegraphic
transmission:

"Unanimous opinion that action cannot be
postponed much longer. Delay disadvantageous to us.
We can now put up an effective fight. Our enemies

cannot allow us much more time. The arrest of our leaders would hamper us severely. Initiative on our part is necessary. The Irish regiments which are in sympathy with us are being gradually replaced by English regiments.

"We have therefore decided to begin action on Easter Saturday. Unless entirely new circumstances arise we must have your arms and munitions in Limerick between Good Friday and Easter Saturday. We expect German help immediately after beginning action. We might be compelled to begin earlier."

The Confidential Agent will advise (the Irish) if at all possible to wait, and will point out the difficulties in the way of (our) giving help, but nevertheless believes that circumstances make delay impossible. The Committee here will come to a decision independently.

War Intelligence Centre,
SKAL

Despatch

Your Excellency, *Berlin, 12th February*, 1916
I have the honour, in answer to your report of the 24th December of last year, to acknowledge the payment of 1,000 dollars to Sir Roger Casement mentioned in wireless telegram.

ZIMMERMAN

The following was attached surreptitiously by Count Bernstorff to a message regarding the "Lusitania" negotiations, which was sanctioned and passed through by the State Department of the American Government, 18th February, 1916.

> The Irish leader, John Devoy, informs me that rising is to begin in Ireland on Easter Saturday. Please send arms to (arrive at) Limerick, west coast of Ireland, between Good Friday and Easter Saturday.
>
> To put it off longer is impossible. Let me know if help may be expected from Germany.
>
> BERNSTORFF

Foreign Office, Berlin, to German Embassy, Washington
4th March, 1916

> In reply to telegram of 17th February. Between 20th and 23rd April, in the evening, two or three steam-trawlers could land 20,000 rifles and 10 machine-guns, with ammunition and explosives at Fenit Pier in Tralee Bay.
>
> Irish pilot-boat to await the trawlers at dusk, north of the Island of Inishtooskert, at the entrance of Tralee Bay, and show two green lights close to each other at short intervals. Please wire whether the necessary arrangements in Ireland can be made secretly through Devoy. Success can only be assured by the most vigorous efforts.

On 12th March, 1916, a code message in German was sent by wireless from the German Embassy in Washington to banker Max Moebius, Oberwallstrasse, Berlin; translated it was:

National Germania Insurance Contract certainly promised. Executor is evidently satisfied with proposition. Necessary steps have been taken.

HENRY NEWMAN

Decoded it reads:

Irish agree to proposition.
Necessary steps have been taken.

German Embassy, Washington, to Foreign Office, Berlin
14*th March*, 1916

The Irish agree. Will follow instructions. Details sent to Ireland by messenger.

Despatch addressed to Mr Z.N.G. Olifiers, 121 Keizergracht 121, Sloterdyk, near Amsterdam, per SS "Noordam" via Rotterdam.

Washington, 15*th March*, 1916

Continuation of telegram

If those fishing steamers are equipped with wireless apparatus, the signals mentioned for the Limerick proposal would come in very useful. They are: for warning that the vessel is coming, "Finn"; for warning that something wrong has happened, "Bran". In case the fishing vessels are not equipped with wireless apparatus, the without wire signal could be sent from Germany and our friends would surely pick them up as they have numerous private receiving stations, though they cannot send out anything. "Bran" sent from Germany would mean

that something had gone wrong, whether delay in
starting or interruption of voyage, and another date
mentioned with this would mean that the affair was
postponed to that date. "Finn" would mean that the
cargo had started on time to arrive about date already
arranged. It is important that they should be able to
make the necessary arrangements in time, and be able
to conscript sufficient force at right moment. They
are quite prepared to take all chances, but want to
prearrange as much as possible to do. In case a
submarine should come into Dublin Bay in
connection with landing of anything, either material
or officers, the signals "Ashling" would ensure
immediate recognition. If a submarine should enter
the Bay unconnected with any expedition no signal
is necessary, and she should go right up to the
Pigeon-house, which is now used as an electric plant,
and a sewage station where boats are constantly
entering and leaving and there are no nets.

JOHN DEVOY
BERNSTOFF

German Embassy, Washington, to Foreign Office, Berlin
March 21st, 1916

In case the trawlers are fitted with wireless, they are
to make the following signals in the Limerick
expedition:
As a sign that ships are coming, "Finn".
As a sign that something untoward has occurred,
"Bran".

If the trawler is not fitted with wireless, then send wireless from Germany. There are numerous private receiving stations in Ireland. "Bran" sent from Germany is to have the meaning that something has gone wrong. The addition of a date means the date to which the expedition has been postponed. "Finn" means that the cargo has left at the right time. If submarines proceed into Dublin Bay in connection with the landing of war material or officers, then the signal is "Ashling".

If only submarines come, no signal is necessary. They are then to go straight up to the Pigeon-house, where they can proceed in and out at any time. No nets have been set.

Foreign Office, Berlin, to German Embassy, Washington
26th March, 1916

Three trawlers and a small cargo steamer are coming with 1,400 tons cargo-measurement. Lighters must be kept in readiness. As at present arranged, Nauer will send out each night at 12 midnight, starting from 8th April, as introduction to its press service, the word "Finn" as a sign that the cargo has started as arranged. The word "Bran" will be sent if there is any hitch. A date placed after "Bran" means that the arrival of the steamer has been postponed to that date. The wave length will be 4,700 meters. I would recommend that the stations should listen for Nauer for practice first. Everything else will be done in accordance with arrangements made.

Despatch

> *Washington, 10th April, 1916*
>
> John Devoy requests that the following telegram may be forwarded to Sir Roger Casement: . . . Should Sir Roger be away or ill, J. D. requests that the telegram be delivered to John Monteith.
>
> BERNSTORFF

Message in envelope addressed to M. H. Eisenhuth, 5, Stationsvej, Gentofte, Copenhagen, per SS "Hellig Olav".

> *Washington, April 12, 1916*
>
> The 500 dollars mentioned in radiogram were also given to me by Devoy to be given to Casement. Please advise of payment.

German Embassy, Washington, to Foreign Office, Berlin

> *18th April, 1916*
>
> Delivery of arms must take place punctually on Sunday, 23rd April, in the evening. This is of the highest importance. As smuggling is impossible, the landing must be carried out rapidly.

German Embassy, Washington, to Foreign Office, Berlin

> *19th April, 1916*
>
> Very Urgent
>
> The Irish desire to know if submarines are coming to Dublin Harbour; if not, do they intend to blockade the harbour, and, if possible, Limerick Harbour?
>
> The landing of a body of troops, however small, is urgently desired, and they further suggest a simultaneous strong demonstration by airships and at sea.

In April 1916 a seizure was made by the United States Government at the office of Wolf von Igel, 60, Wall Street, New York, of certain documents which proved the intimate relations between the accredited representatives of the Kaiser in the United States and Irish plotters against the laws and security of the United States, as well as against the British Empire. Excerpts from them were published by the American Government. As far as they have been already disclosed, they give a glimpse into a portion of the intrigue between the Irish revolutionaries and the German Government. Von Igel had established in the autumn of 1914 what was ostensibly an "advertising agency" in Wall Street. The business carried on there had, however, nothing whatever to do with advertising. He was an official of the German Embassy, and his office was practically a sub-bureau of the German Foreign Office at Washington. Von Igel was specially concerned with the German-Irish intrigues.

German Embassy, Washington, to Foreign Office, Berlin
20th April, 1916

Cohalan requests me to send on the following:

The Irish revolt can only succeed if assisted by Germany, otherwise England will be able to crush it, although after a severe struggle. Assistance required: there would be an air raid on England and a naval attack timed to coincide with the rising, followed by a landing of troops and munitions and also of some officers, perhaps from an airship. It might then be possible to close the Irish harbours against England, set up bases for submarines and cut off food export to England. A successful rising may decide the war.

Foreign Office, Berlin, to German Embassy, Washington
22nd April, 1916

Sending of submarine to Dublin harbour impossible.

VON JAGOW

Casement left Kiel about the 12th April, 1916, in a German submarine, accompanied by Monteith, a dismissed ordnance store conductor. He was an Irish Volunteer organiser who had gone to America and thence to Germany. They landed on the coast of Kerry on Good Friday, 21st April, 1916. Casement was captured; Monteith escaped. A German ship, the "Aud", carrying arms for the rebels, was intercepted by a British cruiser, and her commander sunk the "Aud".

The rebellion broke out in Dublin on Easter Monday, the 24th April, 1916, a day after the scheduled time. It was suppressed upon the 1st May, when the rebels surrendered. On the 24th April—as arranged between the German Government and the Sinn Fein leaders—a Zeppelin raid was made on East Anglia. On the 25th April a German naval raid was made on Lowestoft and Yarmouth, and a Zeppelin raid on Essex and Kent.

The Proclamation of the Provisional Government of the Irish Republic, signed by the rebel leaders, declared that:

> Having organised and trained her manhood through her secret revolutionary organisation, the Irish Republican Brotherhood, and through her open military organisations, the Irish Volunteers and the Irish Citizen Army, having patiently perfected her discipline, having resolutely waited for the right moment to reveal itself, she now seizes that moment, and, supported by her exiled children in America and by gallant Allies in Europe, but relying in the first on her own strength, she strikes in full confidence of victory.

This secret revolutionary organisation was the Irish Republican Brotherhood, or the Clan-na-Gael, which carries on the tradition of the Fenian Brotherhood. From 1861 to 1865 it had been in the process of establishment in America as an Irish Revolutionary Society, and was known to the public as the Fenian or Irish Revolutionary Brotherhood, or IRB. It was subsequently extended through the

Clan-na-Gael. The Clan-na-Gael was composed of a federation of clubs divided into districts, and had, and still has, very wide ramifications in America, and a close connection through the IRB with Ireland. John Devoy, the Fenian leader, had been the Secretary of the Clan-na-Gael for over twenty years, and is its dominant figure.

Among other prominent members is Judge Cohalan, who became a member in 1899, and has been chairman of very many of the biennial conventions held by the organisation. He is an *ex officio* member of the Executive.

Other prominent members were Joseph M'Garrity, of Philadelphia; John T. Ryan of Buffalo; John P. Keating, Jeremiah O'Leary; and his brother, John O'Leary; St John Gaffney, who was formerly United States consul at Dresden and Munich, but dismissed from that office by the United States Government. We find Dr McCartan, Mellowes and Monteith, all of whom fled from Ireland after the rebellion, closely associated with its councils and operations. Kuno Meyer was in touch with the Clan-na-Gael when in America.

The total casualties arising out of the rebellion were as follows:

	Killed	Wounded	Missing	Total
Military officers	17	46		63
other ranks	99	322	9	430
RIC officers	2			2
other ranks	11	22		33
DMP	3	7		10
Civilians and insurgents	318	2,217		2,535
	450	2,614	9	3,073

With the exception of those in the RIC, the only other casualties outside Dublin were eight civilians killed and one military officer and nine civilians wounded.

Field General Courts-Martial were at once constituted for the trial of the prisoners taken in the rebellion; 3,430 men and 79 women were arrested. Of these, 1,424 men and 73 women were released after enquiry. One hundred and seventy men and one woman were tried by Courts-Martial, and of these 159 men and one woman were convicted and the remaining 11 acquitted. The remainder of the prisoners, 1,836 men and five women, were sent to England and interned there.

Of the 160 persons convicted by Courts-Martial:

15 were sentenced to death and executed.

10 were sentenced to penal servitude for life.

1 was sentenced to 20 years' penal servitude.

33 were sentenced to 10 years' penal servitude.

3 were sentenced to 8 years' penal servitude.

1 was sentenced to 7 years' penal servitude.

18 were sentenced to 5 years' penal servitude.

56 were sentenced to 3 years' penal servitude.

2 were sentenced to 2 years' imprisonment
with hard labour.

17 were sentenced to 1 year's imprisonment with
hard labour.

4 were sentenced to 6 months' imprisonment
with hard labour.

The names of the persons executed were:

P. H. Pearse

Thomas McDonagh

Joseph Plunkett

Edmund Kent

Thomas J. Clarke

James Connolly

John McDermott

The above were the seven men who signed the Declaration proclaiming the formation of the Irish Republic. The other prominent leaders executed were:

Edward Daly

William Pearse

Cornelius Colbert

J. J. Heuston

Michael O'Hanrahan

John McBride

Michael Mallin

For the murder of Head Constable Rowe at Fermoy on 2nd May:

Thomas Kent

In all 90 persons were sentenced to death by the Courts-Martial, but in only fifteen cases were the sentences carried out, the sentences in the other cases being commuted to various terms of penal servitude by the GOC-in-Chief.

Of the persons sent to England for internment, 1,272 were subsequently discharged after their cases had been investigated, and later on at Christmas 1916 the remainder were released. In the general amnesty which was granted in June prior to the setting up of the Irish Convention, all persons who were either interned, or undergoing sentences of penal servitude or imprisonment for complicity in the rebellion, were released.

In a letter written by P.H. Pearse the night before his execution the following postscript appeared:

The help I expected from Germany failed; the British sunk the ships.

PART III

∞⊷◈⊶∞

REPORT OF THE ROYAL COMMISSION

ON THE

REBELLION IN IRELAND

1916

The Easter Rising took place from 24th to 29th April 1916. It was led by Patrick Pearse of the Irish Republican Brotherhood, and James Connolly of the socialist citizen armies, and was largely confined to Dublin. The climax of the rebellion was the seizure of the General Post Office. When the uprising was finally suppressed, the extent of the reprisals by the British had the effect of increasing support for Sinn Fein.

A Commission of Inquiry was held by the British Government into the causes of the uprising. This is the text of the report. The main people mentioned in the report were as follows:

On the British side, Augustine Birrell was Chief Secretary for Ireland from 1907 to 1916. He resigned after the Easter Rising of 1916. Sir Matthew Nathan had been appointed Under-Secretary to Ireland in 1914, and he was responsible for political affairs in Ireland.

For the Irish, Eoin or John McNeill, the leader of the Irish Volunteers, reluctantly accepted the insurrection when it happened, but countermanded it when German aid failed. McNeill was to become a prominent member of the new Sinn Fein party. John Redmond was an Irish politician who championed the cause of Home Rule for Ireland. He deplored the Easter Rising, and was an opponent of Sinn Fein.

THE IRISH GOVERNMENT

The executive government of Ireland is entrusted to three officers, namely, the Lord Lieutenant, the Chief Secretary to the Lord Lieutenant, and the Under-Secretary: and for the purpose of maintaining order they have at their disposal two police forces, namely, the Royal Irish Constabulary and the Dublin Metropolitan Police Force. "Theoretically," says Sir William Anson, "the executive government of Ireland is conducted by the Lord Lieutenant in Council, sub-ject to instructions which he may receive from the

Home Office of the United Kingdom. Practically it is conducted for all important purposes by the Chief Secretary to the Lord Lieutenant."

The Lord Lieutenant (who is also Governor-General) is resident in Ireland. By the terms of his patent he is responsible for the civil government of the country, and the naval and military forces of the Crown in Ireland are under his orders. But when the Chief Secretary is in the Cabinet and the Lord Lieutenant is not, all powers and responsibility are in practice vested in the Chief Secretary. His policy is the policy of the British Government as a whole and it is obviously impossible that there should be any other independent authority or responsibility in Ireland. For many years past the office of Lord Lieutenant has been a ceremonial office; apart from the exercise of the prerogative of mercy he has no executive functions. Proclamations, appointments and other State documents are issued in his name, but they are put before him for signature, without previous consultation. He is only furnished with information as to the state of the country which he nominally governs, when he asks for it, and then as a matter of courtesy. The military and naval forces in Ireland take their orders from the War Office and Admiralty respectively.

The office of Chief Secretary is a political office, changing with the Government. The executive Government of Ireland is entirely in his hands subject to the control of the Cabinet. When the Chief Secretary is a member of the Cabinet, as has been the case in recent years, he is, of necessity, to a great extent an absentee from Ireland. He has to attend Cabinet Meetings, and he is the only person who can, with authority, answer questions and defend the Government policy in the House of Commons. Although the Chief Secretary is in the position of a Secretary of State, he has no Parliamentary Under-Secretary, and the Irish law officers are frequently not members of the House of Commons. During the last two and a half years of Birrell's nine years' tenure of office, Parliament has been in almost continuous session. He had, therefore, during this critical period but little opportunity of making himself personally acquainted with the state of affairs in Ireland. He was dependent for information on the reports of his Under-Secretary and the advice given by those Irish Members of Parliament whom he chose to consult.

The Under-Secretary is a civil servant, residing in Ireland. For practical purposes he can only take action under authority delegated to him by the Chief Secretary. His duty is to report fully and fairly to his Chief all information that he can obtain, to give his advice freely as to what should be done, and then loyally to carry out the instructions of this Chief without regard to any personal opinion of his own.

For the ordinary maintenance of law and order the Irish Government have two police forces, viz., the Royal Irish Constabulary and the Dublin Metropolitan Police Force. Both forces are under the direct control of the Irish Government, though a rate is levied in Dublin as a contribution to the expenses of the Dublin force. It appears that since 1905 the Dublin Corporation have refused to pay the proceeds of this rate into the police fund, and that the matter has been adjusted by deducting the amount from the Local Taxation account. The Royal Irish Constabulary is a quasi-military force. Its members are armed with carbines and taught to shoot. They police the whole of Ireland, except the Dublin Police district. When the rebellion broke out the Constabulary were somewhat under strength, as it had furnished a good many recruits to the Army. The military authorities were naturally anxious to get recruits from a body of men with splendid physique and a fine record of honourable service.

The Dublin Police is also a fine body of men and its numbers were also slightly diminished by reason of enlistments. The force is unarmed, consequently when an armed rebellion broke out in Dublin, the police had to be withdrawn from duty. If Dublin, like Cork and Belfast, had been policed by the Royal Irish Constabulary, a thousand armed and disciplined policemen, knowing every nook and cranny of the city, would have been a formidable addition to the thousand soldiers who were available when the rebellion first broke out, and the rebels might have hesitated to face them. As Sir Matthew Nathan expressed it in his letter of the 18th December, 1915, to Mr Birrell, in the event of an outbreak, "Each policeman would be worth three soldiers." It is clear from the evidence that the two police forces work cordially together, but it is obvious that two separate forces, under separate commands, cannot be in a time of emergency as efficient as a single force under one command. Each of the forces has a small special Crimes Branch, drawn from uniformed men. For ordinary police purposes this branch does its work well, but it is not specially qualified to deal with political crime, which takes no notice of the boundaries of police districts, and which in the case of Ireland assumes an international complexion.

If the Irish system of government be regarded as a whole it is anomalous in quiet times, and almost unworkable in times of crisis.

LEGAL POWERS OF THE IRISH EXECUTIVE

The legal powers vested in the Irish Government for the maintenance of law and order, and the suppression of sedition must now be considered.

From 1881 to 1906 the Peace Preservation (Ireland) Act was in force in that country. Under that enactment the Government had complete control over the importation and sale of arms and ammunition, and over the carrying of arms or the possession of ammunition. The Act was a temporary one continued from year to year by the expiring Laws

Continuance Act. In 1906 the Act was allowed to lapse by Sir Henry Campbell Bannerman's Government. But the Irish Government had other, though less efficient, powers for dealing with unauthorised bodies who sought to arm themselves. If the ordinary excise duty on carrying a gun had been enforced a complete register of firearms would have been obtained and the poorer members of the community might have found difficulty in paying the licence duty. It seems that no attempt was made to enforce this law, the only reason alleged being that the people concerned would have refused to take out the licence and pay the duty.

The Explosive Substances Act 1883, which applies to the whole of the United Kingdom, gives drastic powers for dealing with explosives, and it may be assumed that the term "explosive" would include stores of ammunition as well as high explosives. Under that Act, if any person has in his possession any explosive substance he is guilty of felony and liable on conviction to 14 years' penal servitude unless he can show that he was in possession thereof for a lawful object. Accessories are liable to a like punishment. For the purpose of discovering stores of explosives, the Attorney General, if he has reasonable ground for believing that the Act has been disobeyed, may order an inquiry at which witnesses may be examined on oath, although no person is charged with any crime under the Act.

The Unlawful Drilling Act 1819 is an Act "to prevent the training of persons to the use of Arms, and to the practice of Military Evolutions and Exercise." It prohibits drilling and military exercises unless authorised by the Crown, the Lieutenant, or two county justices, and authorises any justice or peace officer to disperse any meeting unauthorised for drilling, and to arrest the persons attending it. As regards procedure, the Criminal Law and Procedure (Ireland) Act 1887, besides providing for special jury trials in proclaimed districts, empowers the Lord Lieutenant by proclamation to prohibit or suppress "dangerous associations" and defines as dangerous any association which (*inter alia*) interferes with the administration of the law or disturbs the maintenance of law and order.

It may be noted too that the old Acts, known as the Whiteboy Acts, some of which were passed by the Irish Parliament, appear to be still in force. These Acts give the Government extensive powers for dealing with riotous or unlawful assemblies.

The Irish Government have also the ordinary common law powers for proceeding against persons who publish seditious libels, or engage in seditious conspiracies. But legal powers are of no avail unless the Government make up their minds to put them into execution, and can rely on juries and magistrates to do their duty when prosecutions are supported by adequate evidence.

War broke out on the 5th August, 1914, and on the 8th August the Defence of the Realm Act 1914 was passed. This Act authorised His Majesty in Council to issue Regulations during the continuance of the war, "for securing the public safety and the defence of the realm" and instituted trial by Court Martial for serious offences against the Regulations. Under these provisions there appeared to be ample powers for dealing with any manifestations of sedition or rebellion. But as regards Ireland, the teeth of this enactment were drawn by the Defence of the Realm Amendment Act 1915 which was passed on the 18th March, 1915. That Act provided that any British subject (not being a person subject to military law) charged with an offence under the Defence of the Realm Act might claim to be tried by a jury in a civil court, instead of by Court Martial. Power was given to His Majesty to suspend the operation of this provision "in the event of invasion or other special military emergency". But it certainly would have been difficult to have justified the exercise of this suspensory power in Ireland before any actual outbreak in arms had occurred. It was impossible, as stated by Mr Birrell and other witnesses, to get a conviction, in any case tried by a jury, for an offence against law and order however strong the evidence for the Crown might be. The power of internment conferred by the Regulations applied primarily to foreigners, and only extended to British subjects when "hostile association" could be established. Therefore, however serious an offence might be, the only remedy was a prosecution before a court of summary jurisdiction where six months' imprisonment was the maximum punishment that could be imposed, and when a case was tried before justices, there was no certainty that the decision would be in accordance with the evidence.

CAUSES OF THE OUTBREAK

In dealing with the series of events which led up to
the outbreak of the 24th April, 1916, and in endeavouring to elucidate the causes of the rebellion in
Ireland, the fact should be borne in mind that there is
always a section of opinion in that country bitterly
opposed to the British connection, and that at times
of excitement this section can impose its sentiments
on largely disinterested members of the people. As Mr
Birrell described it:

The spirit of what today is called Sinn Feinism is
mainly composed of the old hatred and distrust of
the British connection, always noticeable in all classes,
and in all places, varying in degree, and finding
different ways of expression, but always there as the
background of Irish Politics and character.

The incidents which preceded the rising in April,
1916, are fully detailed in the evidence of the witnesses, but may be summarised as follows. In the
winter of 1913, while industrial strikes were in
progress in Dublin, an armed force of working men,
officially called the Citizen Army, was first created. As
this force was partly armed, and the Dublin
Metropolitan Police are an unarmed force, the
employers were in some cases compelled to arm their
carters to resist intimidation by the strikers. This
lawless display of force should have been a warning
against the recent policy of permitting the indiscriminate arming of civilians in Ireland in times of
turbulence and faction. In periods of peace it may
be desirable in an orderly community to disregard
some seditious utterances as mere vapouring, but
when a country is engaged in a serious struggle,
sedition alters its aspect and becomes treason, dangerous to the community, and should promptly be
suppressed. As stated by Sir David Harrel in his
evidence,

the Irish people are easily led, and it is therefore the
more incumbent on Government to nip lawlessness

and disorder in the bud. Neglect in this respect has invariably led to things getting out of hand, with the result that strong repressive measures become necessary and much hardship is imposed upon misled, but perhaps comparatively inoffensive, people.

On the 13th December, 1913, in view of information that arms were entering the province of Ulster from foreign countries, including Germany, a Proclamation was issued under the Customs Consolidation Act 1876, prohibiting the importation of arms into Ireland. In defiance of this, large quantities of arms were surreptitiously imported by night at Larne and other places in April, 1914. Before this date other similar consignments had been seized and confiscated. It has been stated that as a matter of policy it was decided by the Government not to take proceedings against those responsible for this breach of the law. The validity of the Proclamation was afterwards questioned in an action brought by a gunsmith of Ulster against the Customs authorities, but on the 15th June, 1914, a majority of an Irish Court upheld its validity. Notwithstanding this decision the Irish Government decided to withdraw the Proclamation, and the withdrawal, though decided on before the outbreak of the War, was publicly notified on the 5th August, 1914, the day after war broke out.

On Sunday, the 26th July, 1914, a large consignment of arms and ammunition from abroad was landed at Howth, near Dublin, for the use of the Irish National Volunteers, who will be hereafter described.

Members of that force overpowered the Customs Officers and landed and distributed the arms. An attempt was made by the Dublin Metropolitan Police, acting under orders of Mr W. V. Harrel, the Assistant Commissioner, to enforce the Proclamation by seizure. After trying fruitlessly to obtain the co-operation of a detachment of the Royal Irish Constabulary he called in a military force to assist him, and a few of the arms were taken, but most of the Volunteers retired with the weapons before the arrival of the military.

Whilst the troops were returning to barracks they were attacked by a mob and an unfortunate incident occurred by which some members of the public lost their lives through shots from the soldiers in Bachelor's Walk. Mr Harrel was immediately suspended by the Chief Secretary pending further investigation. A Royal Commission was appointed to enquire into this matter, and sat from the 6th to the 11th August, 1914. In their report which was submitted to Your Majesty, Mr Harrel was censured by the Commission for his conduct in invoking the assistance of the troops, and he resigned his position. The Chief Commissioner Sir John Ross, of Bhadensburg, had previously resigned his position after the order of temporary suspension had been issued against Mr Harrel. The resignation of Mr Harrel was looked upon by the public in Dublin as tantamount to dismissal, and while it appears that it had no effect on the loyalty of the Dublin Metropolitan Police, it tended to discourage the officers of that body from initiative in enforcing the law. Further, there can be no doubt that his dismissal tended to weaken the authority of the police, as it gave rise to the opinion amongst the more ignorant classes that in any case of disorder the Government might not support their action.

In spite of the breach of the Proclamation of December 1913 in the landing of arms at Howth, the Irish Government decided (as in the case of the arms imported at Larne) to take no action, and to institute no prosecution, and on the 5th August, as has been above stated, the restriction upon the importation of arms into Ireland was removed.

From the evidence given before the Royal Commission it is clear that the insurrection was caused by two bodies of men allied together for this purpose and known as the Irish Volunteers and the Citizen Army. It is now a matter of common notoriety that the Irish Volunteers have been in communication with the authorities in Germany and were for a long time known to be supplied with money through Irish-American societies. This was stated in public by Mr John McNeill on the 8th November, 1914. It was suspected long before the outbreak that some of the money came from German forces.

The following facts show what was known of the origin and development of these two bodies and the action taken by the Irish Government in dealing with their activities.

The Irish National Volunteers owed their origin to a meeting at Dublin in November 1913 of twelve men who came together to discuss the formation of an Irish Volunteer Army. The founders of the force included John McNeill, Bulmer Hobson, F.H. Pearse and the O'Rahillys. After the decision to enrol volunteers had been taken, a meeting attended by some thousands of people was held in Dublin and the movement took shape. It was started quite independently of any Irish political party by men strongly opposed to any political connection of Ireland with England. By June 1914, 65,000 men were reported to have been enrolled and Mr Redmond in that month succeeded in securing the addition of enough members to the Committee to secure to himself and his party the control of the movements of the body, to the great dissatisfaction of the original founders.

On the eve of the Prime Minister's meeting in Dublin on 25th September, 1914—where Mr Redmond spoke strongly in favour of recruiting—a manifesto was issued attacking Mr Redmond's attitude. This was signed by McNeill and six others (afterwards involved in the Rebellion) and concluded by regretting that Roger Casement's absence prevented his being a signatory. On 30th September this party disassociated themselves from the Irish National Volunteers and formed a new force called the Irish Volunteers. By the end of October the force enrolled numbered over 13,000 including 2,000 in Dublin. Of these, more than 8,000 were known to be actively engaged in drilling at the end of 1914, and to be in possession of over 1,400 rifles.

It was of paramount importance after the outbreak of the present war that no opportunity should have been given for the drilling and arming of any body of men known to be of seditious tendency, and no other consideration should have interfered with the enforcing of this duty. After the war broke out there was a considerable wave of feeling in Ireland in favour of the Allies. Reservists joining the Colours were greeted with enthusiasm and recruiting was successful. It was owing to the activities of the leaders of the Sinn Fein movement that the forces of disloyalty gradually and steadily increased, and undermined the initial sentiment of patriotism.

The words "Sinn Fein" (ourselves alone) rather describe a movement than an association and the principal efforts of those connected with the movement before the outbreak of the war had been active opposition to any recruiting of Irishmen for the British Army and Navy, and a passive opposition to all Irish parliamentary parties. From the fact that some leaders of the Sinn Fein also led the Irish Volunteers, the latter have frequently been called the Sinn Fein Volunteers, and the two expressions from the end of 1914 are synonymous.

Between the 5th August, 1914, and the 5th December, 1914, there was no law in force prohibiting the importation of arms into Ireland. Certain warrants had been issued by the Lord Lieutenant, authorising the police to seize arms, but on the 5th December, an amendment of the Regulations under the Defence of the Realm Act empowered the police to seize arms and explosives which might be landed on the coast, an exception being made in favour of sporting shot guns, which was, however, cancelled on the 5th February, 1915. Nevertheless arms and explosives continued to be smuggled into Ireland. A flood of seditious literature was disseminated by the leaders of the Irish Volunteer Party early in the War and certain newspapers were suppressed, but according to the statement of the Under-Secretary for Ireland, action against the seditious press was not very consistently taken, and prominent members of the Irish Parliamentary Party were strongly against newspaper suppression.

By the end of March, 1915, the Irish Volunteers do not appear to have increased much in numbers although they had acquired more arms. On 16th March, 1915, the Defence of the Realm Act, Number 2, was passed, by which any British subject could claim the right to trial by jury for an offence against the Defence of the Realm Regulations, and this Act to a great extent hampered the Irish Executive in dealing with cases of sedition in Ireland. Insufficient attention appears to have been paid to the state of affairs in Ireland in both Houses of Parliament.

Throughout the whole of the remainder of the year 1915 the Irish Volunteer Party were active in their efforts to encourage sedition. Seditious papers were published, pamphlets of a violent tone issued and circulated, paid organisers were sent throughout the country to enrol and drill volunteer recruits, and the leaders themselves were active in attending anti-recruiting meetings at which disloyal speeches were openly made. A considerable number of the younger members of the priesthood in certain districts joined in the movement and schoolmasters who were followers of the Sinn Fein movement disseminated treason amongst the younger people through the medium of the Irish language.

Action was taken during this period against seditious newspapers and against certain paid organisers of the Irish Volunteer Party, but this course was strongly opposed by members of the Irish Parliamentary Party and the Nationalist press. Major Price in his evidence says:

> One unfortunate thing which hindered us a good
> deal was the attitude of the official Nationalist Party
> and their press. Whenever General Friend did
> anything strong in the way of suppressing or
> deporting these men (the organisers) from Ireland,
> they at once deprecated it, and said it was a
> monstrous thing to turn a man out of Ireland.

Irishmen no doubt appreciate the maintenance of order, but they appear to have an inveterate prejudice against the punishment of disorder.

So seditious had the country become during 1915 that juries in Dublin and magistrates in various parts of the country through fear or favour could not be trusted to give decisions in accordance with the evidence. The only tribunals which could be relied upon at this time were those presided over by resident

and of the Chief Commissioner of
Metropolitan Police, to show that e
outbreak of war and during the w
of the existing state of affairs
Under-Secretary, and thro
Secretary. On the 15th Ju
mitted from the offic
which it was stated

In Ireland
of a g
de

and ability. By the month of November, 1915, it was
known that the two bodies were acting in combina-
tion in Dublin.

In the newspaper *The Workers' Republic*, edited by
James Connolly, the following passage occurs:

> The Irish Citizen Army was the first publicly
> organised, armed citizen body south of the Bevan. Its
> constitution pledged and still pledges its members to
> work for an Irish Republic and for the emancipation
> of labour.

Before turning to the events of the present year it is
desirable to refer to the confidential reports of the
Inspector-General of the Royal Irish Constabulary

the Dublin
ven before the
ar, full knowledge
was supplied to the
gh him to the Chief
ne, 1914, a report was sub-
e of the Inspector-General in

the training and drilling to the use of arms
eat part of the male population is a new
parture which is bound in the not too distant
future to alter all the existing conditions of life.
Obedience to the law has never been a prominent
characteristic of the people. In times of passion or
excitement the law has only been maintained by
force, and this has been rendered practicable owing to
the want of cohesion among the crowds hostile to
the police. If the people become armed and drilled
effective police control will vanish. Events are
moving. Each county will soon have a trained army
for outnumbering the police, and those who control
the Volunteers will be in a position to dictate to
what extent the law of the land may be carried into
effect.

As early as the 7th September, 1914, the Dublin
Metropolitan Police were warning the Government
of the danger to be expected within Dublin itself. On
that date the following statement was made to the
Government:

There is no doubt that so far as Dublin is concerned the majority of the Irish National Volunteers would follow the lead of the extreme section and hints have been given that they are not without hope of being able to assume and establish control of the Government of Ireland before the present difficulties are over and that they may attempt some escapade before long.

On the 26th October, 1914, the Detective Department of the Dublin Metropolitan Police submitted to the Under-Secretary notes of the speeches made by the Irish Volunteers at their first Annual Convention. The demonstrators had marched to the meeting nearly 1,000 strong, 230 of their number armed with rifles and 20 of the National Boy Scouts similarly equipped. Speeches of the most inflammatory and revolutionary character were delivered. The leaders predicted rebellion and the shedding of blood in the great fight of Ireland against the British Empire.

These documents were seen by the Chief Secretary, but he wrote no comment on their contents, and no proceedings were taken.

From the commencement the Dublin Metropolitan Police were in all respects as diligent as the Royal Irish Constabulary in forwarding to the Government regular information as to the conduct and progress of the hostile organisations within their jurisdiction.

In the Annual Report of the Inspector-General delivered at the end of the year 1914 the following words occur:

In the personnel of the Committee in its declaration of policy, in the utterances of its leading representatives in the Press, and at public meetings, in its opposition to the efforts of Mr Redmond and the Irish Parliamentary Party to bring Ireland into line at the present national crisis, and in its crusade against enlistment in the Army, the Irish Volunteer organisation has shown itself to be disloyal, seditious and revolutionary, if the means and opportunity were at hand.

On the 12th February, 1915, a further report was submitted, in which it was stated that at certain meetings of the Irish Republican Brotherhood in Tyrone members were reminded of the opportunity afforded by the present crisis to strike a blow for the independence of Ireland, and they were promised arms and ammunition when the time arrived.

At certain places in Co. Wexford after the promulgation of military orders under the Defence of the Realm Act for the action of the inhabitants in the event of an invasion, counter notices were placarded calling on the people to disobey the orders issued and to welcome the German troops as friends.

In a report submitted on the 13th July, 1915, it was stated that information had been received from a reliable source that a sum of 3,000 dollars had been recently sent from America to the Council of the Irish Volunteers.

In a report submitted on the 14th September, 1915, the following passage occurs:

According to the information confidentially obtained, communications are passing between the leaders of the Clan-na-Gael in America and the Sinn Fein in Ireland, and money has been sent over to the latter to help them in a campaign of disloyalty. As the leaders of the Irish Volunteers apparently aim at National Independence, the force bears resemblance to the old Fenian movement, but unlike the latter is ready to drill and arm its members and is not regarded as a secret society. As already reported, according to the confidential information, at a meeting of the Council of Irish Volunteers held in Dublin on the 30th May, 1915, Professor McNeill in the chair, a resolution in favour of the Irish Volunteers declaring themselves in favour of immediate insurrection, proposed by Bulmer Hobson, was only defeated by the casting vote of Professor McNeill.

A report dated the 13th November, 1915, contained the following statement:

This force is disloyal and bitterly Anti-British and is daily improving its organisation. Some drill is practised but its activities are mainly directed to promoting sedition and hindering recruitment for the Army and it is now pledged to resist conscription with arms. According to information from a reliable source the Sinn Feinners have already planned a rising in the event of conscription, and as this is perhaps the one object in which they would find many Redmondites in agreement with them, they might give a serious amount of trouble.

On the 14th December, 1915, a report was submitted that:

> The Irish Volunteers were very active during the month and gained 1,300 new members. Lieutenant O'Leary, VC, was hooted and insulted by a party of Volunteers route marching. A party of 800 held military manoeuvres at Artane, Co. Dublin. The liberty of action at present enjoyed by the openly disloyal and hostile Sinn Feiners is having a very undesirable effect.

On the 29th November, 1915, a special report was delivered which deserves study. It contains the following statement:

> It is a fact that this body of Irish Volunteers numbering 10,000 strong in the provinces with control of 1,500 rifles and possibly more, thoroughly disloyal and hostile to the British Government, is apparently now on the increase and I desire to point out that it might rapidly assume dimensions sufficient to cause anxiety to the military authorities. As it is in the event of an invasion, or of any important reverse to our troops in the field, the Irish Volunteer Force would seriously embarrass arrangements for home defence.

In addition to the information contained in the above-mentioned reports of the Royal Irish Constabulary, Lord Midleton in November 1915 had an interview with the Chief Secretary in which he strongly urged that Irish Volunteers should be disarmed and not permitted to parade, and he pressed for the prosecution of those responsible for seditious speeches. His warnings were entirely neglected.

On the 18th December, 1915, a letter was sent by the Under-Secretary to the Chief Secretary, of which the following passage is an extract:

What is Redmond up to with his comparisons between Ireland and Great Britain in the matters of Police and Crime? He knows, or should know after what Dillon wrote to him over a month ago in the enclosed "confidential" letter and repeated verbally on the 3rd inst., that the present situation in Ireland is most serious and menacing. Redmond himself sent me the other "private" enclosure on the 9th. He knows or should know that the enrolled strength of the Sinn Fein Volunteers has increased by a couple of thousand active members in the last two months to a total of some 13,500 and each group of these is a centre of revolutionary propaganda. He knows, or should know, that efforts are being made to get arms for the support of this propaganda, that the Irish Volunteers already have some 2,500 rifles, and they have their eyes on the 10,000 in the hands of the supine National Volunteers and that they are endeavouring to supplement their rifles with shot guns, revolvers and pistols.

New measures possible requiring additional police at the ports will be required to counter these attempts and unless in other matters we keep these revolutionaries under observation we shall not be in a position to deal with the outbreak, which we hope will not occur, but which undoubtedly will follow any attempt to enforce conscription, or, even if there is no such attempt, might take place as a result of continual unsuccess of the British Arms.

On the 8th January, 1915, Lord Midleton called attention in the House of Lords to the condition of Ireland. In the course of his evidence he said:

I also named four seditious newspapers, and pressed the Government to oppose them, and to say exactly what was the status of the Irish Volunteers. Lord Crewe's reply, which I hand in, minimised the increase of the organisation, expressed sanguine hopes that regulations issued by the military authorities would practically put a stop to this dissemination of seditious newspapers and undertook, under renewed pressure from me, that the full attention of the Irish Government and the military authorities would be given to the status of the Volunteers.

Lord Midleton further said:

On the 26th January, 1916, I had an interview with

the Prime Minister by appointment, and I brought all these facts before him. The Prime Minister asked me to hand him a memorandum giving the views which had been placed into my hands, into which he undertook to make most careful examination. I sent him subsequently at his wish a memorandum which I produce.

He added:

I had an appointment with the Prime Minister for the 14th March on another very important subject, and I proposed then to lay before him the Report of this Committee (which had met to discuss this subject) and to give him a copy of it. Unfortunately the Prime Minister was taken ill on the 13th and subsequently had to go to Rome. In the result the interview never took place.

Besides the warnings above mentioned Lord Midleton gave further warnings at later periods. In his evidence he stated that on 29th February he saw Sir Matthew Nathan and on 6th March Lord Wimborne, and that:

All the questions which had been discussed before were brought up at this meeting and Sir Matthew Nathan especially pressed on me that since our previous interview the movement had been developing much more seriously in Dublin. He mentioned to me the names of those who were

known to the Government as the chief conspirators
and urged me to read as a specimen an article by
Sheehy Skeffington in the January or February
number of the *Century*. I felt so strongly that Sir
Matthew had not the necessary powers that I asked
the Lord Lieutenant of Ireland whether I could go
over and see him and as he was in London he was
good enough to arrange a meeting with me on 6th
March in Arlington Street. I found Lord Wimborne
took rather a more favourable view of the position in
Ireland than Sir Matthew Nathan . . . but the general
trend of the conversation showed that he was most
anxious to deal with some of the ringleaders and I
gathered, although he did not say so in words, he was
unable to move further owing to the general attitude
of the Government towards Ireland which it was
impossible to disturb.

Between January 1916 and the outbreak of the insurrection, the Irish Volunteers steadily increased in
numbers and discipline. During this time they were
known to be supplying themselves with quantities of
arms and high explosives by theft, or otherwise, when
opportunity offered. In the early months of the year
the state of various parts of the country were known
to be lawless. In January the heads of the Royal Irish
Constabulary submitted to the Under-Secretary sug-
gestions for the amendment of the Defence of the
Realm Act and Regulations. They pointed out that
trial by jury had proved to be a failure and that in
many parts of Ireland the magistrates could not be

relied upon to enforce the existing Regulations. A conference was held at the Castle to consider these recommendations early in February. Amendments of the law and prohibition of the carrying of arms by the Irish Volunteers was suggested as remedial measures in a carefully written paper of recommendations submitted to the conference. It was attended by Mr O'Connell, Deputy Inspector-General of the Royal Irish Constabulary and the Under-Secretary General Friend, and the Solicitor-General. The only suggestion discussed was that dealing with explosives—the more serious matters were not even brought forward. Upon this point Mr O'Connell remarked: "It was the impression, rightly or wrongly, that they had been discussed by higher authorities."

The publication of newspapers containing seditious articles continued during the spring of 1916. A number of seditious books called *Tracts for the Times* were circulated. Major Price, of the Army Intelligence Department, informed the Commission that he had consultations with regard to this matter, but added: "I likened myself to John the Baptist preaching in the Wilderness as to taking steps on the subject. The Civil Authorities do not think it desirable to take steps."

On St Patrick's Day, the 17th March, there was a parade of the Irish Volunteers throughout the Provinces under orders from their headquarters. About 4,500 turned out, of whom 1,817 were armed. The report of the Inspector-General of the Royal Irish Constabulary, dealing with this parade, contained the following remarks:

There can be no doubt that the Irish Volunteer leaders are a pack of rebels who would proclaim their independence in the event of any favourable opportunity, but with their present resources and without substantial reinforcements it is difficult to imagine that they will make even a brief stand against a small body of troops. These observations, however, are made with reference to the provinces and not to the Dublin Metropolitan area, which is the centre of the movement.

At the end of last March the Council of the Irish Volunteers assembled in Dublin, and issued a manifesto warning the public that the Volunteers:

cannot submit to be disarmed, and that the raiding for arms and the attempted disarming of men, therefore, in the natural course of things can only be met by resistance and bloodshed.

On the 7th April, 1916, public meetings of the Irish Volunteers were held for the very purpose of protesting against the deportation orders and to enlist recruits. The speeches were very violent, threats being used that persons attempting to disarm the Volunteers would be "shot dead".

The Chief Commissioner made a report to the Under-Secretary, and that document shows clearly the view that Colonel Edgeworth-Johnstone took of the situation:

These recruiting meetings are a very undesirable development and are I think causing both annoyance and uneasiness among loyal citizens . . . The Sinn Fein party are gaining in numbers, in equipment, in discipline and in confidence, and I think drastic action should be taken to limit their activities. The longer this is postponed the more difficult it will be to carry out.

This report reached the Under-Secretary on the 10th April, who wrote on it "Chief Secretary and the Lord Lieutenant to see the Chief Commissioner's minute." On the 12th the Chief Secretary wrote upon it, "Requires careful consideration. Is it thought practicable to undertake a policy of disarmament and, if so, within what limits, if any, can such a policy be circumscribed?" Upon the same day the Lord Lieutenant wrote upon it: "This is a difficult point: could the disarming be satisfactorily effected?"

No answer to the minute was returned to the Royal Irish Constabulary, and the file did not find its way back to the Inspector-General until 24th May.

For some months before the rising, a newspaper campaign was carried on suggesting that if an attempt were made by the Government to disarm the Irish Volunteers, it could only arise from the deliberate intention of Englishmen to provoke disorder and bloodshed. There is no doubt that these articles were intended to intimidate the Irish Government, and to prevent their taking active repressive measures.

On the 18th April news reached Dublin Castle that a ship had left Germany for Ireland on 12th April accompanied by two German submarines, but the news was accompanied by a caution as to its accuracy. The statement added that the ship was due to arrive on the 21st and that a rising was timed for Easter Eve. On the 19th April a special meeting of the Dublin Corporation was held at the Mansion House to discuss the police rate. Alderman Thomas Kelly, in the course of a speech attacking Mr Justice Kenny (who had alluded at the opening of his Commission to the state of disorder in Dublin and had urged military action), made a statement to the effect that he had received that morning from the Editor of *New Ireland* a circular which he would read. It was from a man named Little, of New Ireland Office, 13, Fleet Street, Dublin, dated 16th April, 1916:

> Sir,
> The gravity of the present situation in Ireland
> compels me to invite your serious attention to the
> enclosed. It is a copy of a portion of a document
> recently addressed to, and on the files in, Dublin
> Castle. In view of the deliberate intention here
> revealed on the part of the Government to cause
> bloodshed in Ireland by an attack on the Irish
> Volunteers, a body formed openly in pre-war times
> in a manner certain to provoke armed resistance, I
> appeal to you to use your influence, public and
> private, in whatever manner you may consider would
> best benefit this country. The cipher from which this

document is copied does not indicate punctuation or capitals.

The following precautionary measures have been sanctioned by the Irish Office on the recommendation of the General Officer Commanding the Forces in Ireland. All preparations will be made to put these measures in force immediately on receipt of an Order issued from the Chief Secretary's Office, Dublin Castle, and signed by the Under-Secretary and the General Officer commanding the Forces in Ireland. First, the following persons to be placed under arrest: all members of the Sinn Fein National Council, the Central Executive Irish Sinn Fein Volunteers, General Council Irish Sinn Fein Volunteers, County Board Irish Sinn Fein Volunteers, Executive Committee National Volunteers, Coisde Gnota Committee Gaelic League—see list A3 and 4 and supplementary list A2 . . .

Dublin Metropolitan Police and Royal Irish Constabulary forces in Dublin City will be confined to barracks under the direction of the Competent Military Authority. An order will be issued to inhabitants of city to remain in their houses until such time as the Competent Military Authority may otherwise direct or permit. Pickets chosen from units of Territorial Forces will be placed at all points marked on maps 3 and 4. Accompanying mounted patrols will continuously visit all points and report every hour.

The following premises will be occupied by adequate forces, and all necessary measures used without need of reference to headquarters. First, premises known as Liberty Hall, Beresford Place; No. 6 Harcourt Street, Sinn Fein Building; No. 2 Dawson Street, Headquarters, Volunteers; No. 12 D'Olier Street, Nationality Office; No. 25, Rutland Square, Gaelic League Office; No. 41, Rutland Square, Forester's Hall; Sinn Fein Volunteer premises in the city; all National Volunteer premises in the city; Trades Council premises, Cap 1 Street; Surrey House, Leinster Road, Rathmines.

The following premises will be isolated, and all communications to or from prevented: premises known as Archbishop's house, Drumconda; Mansion House, Dawson Street; No. 40 Herbert Park; Larkfield, Kimmage Road; Woodtown Park, Ballyboden; Saint Enda's College, Hermitage, Rathfarnham; and in addition premises in list 5D, see maps 3 and 4.

Alderman Kelly, in continuing, said that the document was evidently genuine, and that he had done a public service in drawing attention to it, in order to prevent these military operations being carried on in a city which he declared was under God the most peaceable in Europe.

This document was an entire fabrication. Copies of it found since the outbreak are shown by identification of type to have been printed at Liberty Hall, the headquarters of the Citizen Army. It is not known who was the author of this invention or whether Mr Little was in any way responsible for it. Many copies of this forged document were printed and distributed, and it was widely considered by the people to be genuine, and no doubt led to the belief by the members of the Irish Volunteers and Citizen Army that they would shortly be disarmed. This undoubtedly became one of the proximate causes of the outbreak.

On the 22nd April, 1916, the news of the capture of the German ship and of the arrest of a man believed to be Sir Roger Casement was published. The *Irish Volunteer* newspaper announced in its issue of that day under the title of *Headquarters' Bulletin*:

> Arrangements are now nearing completion in all the more important brigade areas for the holding of a very interesting series of manoeuvres at Easter. In some instances the arrangements contemplate a one or two day bivouac. As for Easter, the Dublin programme may well stand as a model for other areas.

Reference was also made to a more elaborate series of manoeuvres at Whitsuntide.

It is clear that the leaders of the movement expected the arrival of the ship, since emissaries of the Irish Volunteers were sent to meet it. The vessel, however, and Sir Roger Casement, appear to have arrived a little sooner than was expected.

On the news of the capture of the ship, orders were given at the headquarters of the Irish Volunteers cancelling throughout all Ireland the arrangements for the following day, Sunday. The order was signed "McNeill, Chief of Staff". This appeared in the early evening papers of Saturday, 22nd April.

In the evening of the 22nd it was known to the authorities that the man arrested was Sir Roger Casement. A conference was held at Dublin Castle on the same evening. The abandonment of the parade of the Volunteers for Sunday was then known. No movements of the Volunteers took place on that day. A report was received on Sunday afternoon that there had been a robbery under arms at about 8 a.m. of 250 lb of gelignite from quarries a few miles south-west of Dublin and that it was believed the stolen material, or part of it, had been taken to Liberty Hall.

Conferences held during Sunday, the 23rd April, at the Castle are fully detailed in the evidence of Lord Wimborne, Sir Matthew Nathan and other witnesses. It was eventually decided that the proper course was to arrest all the leaders of the movement, there being by this time clear evidence of their "hostile associations", but it was agreed that before this could safely be done, military preparations sufficient to overawe armed opposition should be secured.

Early in the morning of the 24th April the Chief Secretary's concurrence with the proposed arrest and internment in England of the hostile leaders was asked for and obtained, but before any further effective steps could be taken the insurrection had broken out and by noon many portions of the City of Dublin had been simultaneously occupied by rebellious armed forces.

There is no doubt that the outbreak had been carefully planned beforehand. A pocket-book discovered upon one of the rebels who took part in the rising in Wexford contained a list of the places actually seized in Dublin when the outbreak occurred.

CONCLUSIONS

It is outside the scope of Your Majesty's instructions for us to enquire how far the policy of the Irish Executive was adopted by the Cabinet as a whole, or to attach responsibility to any but the Civil and Military Executive in Ireland, but the general conclusion that we draw from the evidence before us is that the main cause of the rebellion appears to be that lawlessness was allowed to grow up unchecked, and that Ireland for several years past had been administered on the principle that it was safer and more expedient to leave law in abeyance if collision with any faction of the Irish people could thereby be avoided.

Such a policy is the negation of that cardinal rule of Government which demands that the enforcement of law and the preservation of order should always be independent of political expediency.

We consider that the importation of large quantities of arms into Ireland after the lapse of the Arms Act, and the toleration of drilling by large bodies of men first in Ulster, and then in other districts of Ireland, created conditions which rendered possible the recent troubles in Dublin and elsewhere. It appears to us that reluctance was shown by the Irish Government to repress by prosecution written and spoken seditious utterances, and to suppress the drilling and manoeuvring of armed forces known to be under the control of men who were openly declaring their hostility to Your Majesty's Government and their readiness to welcome and assist Your Majesty's enemies.

This reluctance was largely prompted by the pressure brought to bear by the Parliamentary representatives of the Irish people, and in Ireland itself there developed a widespread belief that no repressive measures would be undertaken by the Government against sedition. This led to a rapid increase of preparations for insurrection and was the immediate cause of the recent outbreak.

We are of the opinion that from the commencement of the present war all seditious utterances and publications should have been firmly suppressed at the outset, and if juries or magistrates were found unwilling to enforce this policy further powers should have been invoked under the existing Acts for the Defence of the Realm.

We are also of the opinion that on the outbreak of war all drilling and manoeuvring by unrecognised bodies of men, whether armed or unarmed, should have been strictly prohibited, and that as soon as it became known to the Irish Government that the Irish Volunteers and the Citizen Army were under the control of men prepared to assist Your Majesty's enemies if the opportunity should be offered to them, all drilling and open carrying of arms by these bodies of men should have been forcibly suppressed.

It does not appear to be disputed that the authorities in the spring of 1916, while believing that the seditious bodies would not venture unaided to break into insurrection, were convinced that they were prepared to assist a German landing.

We are further of the opinion that at the risk of a collision early steps should have been taken to arrest and prosecute leaders and organisers of sedition.

For the reasons given before, we do not think that any responsibility rests upon the Lord Lieutenant. He was appointed in February 1915, and was in no way answerable for the policy of the Government. We are, however, of the opinion that the Chief Secretary, as the administrative head of Your Majesty's Government in Ireland, is primarily responsible for the situation that was allowed to arise and the outbreak that occurred.

Sir Matthew Nathan assumed office as Under-Secretary to the Irish Government in September

1914, only. In our view he carried out with the utmost loyalty the policy of the Government and of his immediate superior the Chief Secretary, but we consider that he did not sufficiently impress upon the Chief Secretary during the latter's prolonged absences from Dublin the necessity for more active measures to remedy the situation in Ireland which on December 18th last in a letter to the Chief Secretary he described as "most serious and menacing".

We are satisfied that Sir Neville Chamberlain, the Inspector-General of the Royal Irish Constabulary, and Colonel Edgworth-Johnstone, the Chief Commissioner of the Dublin Metropolitan Police, required their subordinates to furnish, and did receive from their subordinates, full and exact reports as to the nature, progress and aims of the various armed associations in Ireland. From these sources the Government had abundant material on which they could have acted many months before the leaders themselves contemplated any actual rising.

For the conduct, zeal and loyalty of the Royal Irish Constabulary and the Dublin Metropolitan Police we have nothing but praise.

We do not attach any responsibility to the military authorities in Ireland for the rebellion or its results. As long as Ireland was under civil government these authorities had nothing to do with the suppression of sedition. Their duties were confined to securing efficiency in their own ranks and to the promotion of recruiting, and they could only aid in the suppression of disorder when duly called on by the civil power. By the middle of 1915, it was obvious to the military authorities that their efforts in favour of recruiting were being frustrated by the hostile activities of the Sinn Fein supporters, and they made representations to the Government to that effect. The general danger of the situation was clearly pointed out to the Irish Government by the military authorities, on their own initiative, in February last, but the warning fell on unheeding ears.

In conclusion, we desire to place on record our high appreciation of the services rendered with ability and energy by our Honorary Secretary. For several months Mr Grimwood Mears gave his services voluntarily to the Government in their investigation into cases of alleged German atrocities, and subsequently served as joint Honorary Secretary to the Committee on alleged German outrages, generally known as Lord Bryce's Committee. The experience thus gained by him has been of great advantage to Your Majesty's Commissioners. We offer our cordial thanks to the Secretary of the Commission for the assistance he has given us in the performance of our task.

All which we humbly submit and report for Your Majesty's gracious consideration.

26th June, 1916   HARDINGE OF PENSHURST

MONTAGUE SHEARMAN

MACKENZIE DALZELL CHALMERS

E GRIMWOOD MEARS

Secretary

PART IV

❧

REPORT OF THE ROYAL COMMISSION

ON THE

ARREST ON 25TH APRIL, 1916 AND SUBSEQUENT TREATMENT

OF

MR FRANCIS SHEEHY SKEFFINGTON MR THOMAS DICKSON AND MR PATRICK JAMES McINTYRE

On the day after the outbreak of disturbances in Dublin (which began on Easter Monday), martial law was declared. The following unfortunate incident involving the British Army and three innocent civilians took place, which served to augment the wave of anti-British feeling that was sweeping the country. Both Sheehy Skeffington and his wife were well-known figures in Dublin; she was a campaigner for Women's Rights, and he was an experienced journalist.

The matter later became the subject of a trial, which eventually was followed by an inquiry. This is the text of the report of that inquiry.

The Barracks of Portobello were, on the 24th April 1916, occupied by the 3rd Reserve Battalion of the Royal Irish Rifles. The battalion was commanded by Lieut.-Colonel McCammond, but he was unfortunately on sick leave from 22nd to 29th April, and in his absence the command devolved upon Major Rosborough.

The insurrection broke out early on the 24th of April, and at noon on that day many buildings and places in the city were occupied by the rebels. When the knowledge of the rising spread through the city officers and soldiers on leave repaired to the nearest barracks and reported for duty, and consequently at

Portobello Major Rosborough had under his command many officers and men who were quite unknown to him, but of whose services he was glad to avail himself in the restoration of order.

The Portobello Barracks lie outside the city boundary of Dublin on the south side, being bounded on the north by the Grand Canal, on the east by the Rathmines Road, and on the south by the suburb of Rathmines. The barracks cover a very large area (about 40 acres) and were built for the accommodation of two Infantry Battalions, but at the time of the insurrection not more than 600 men were quartered there, and of these quite half would be on duty outside the barracks. On the 24th and 25th April, various alarming rumours were current as to an impending attack on the barracks and as to various alleged successes of the rebel forces, and undoubtedly at the time both officers and men thought that they were in serious peril, which could only be averted by taking strong measures for the safety of the troops and the barracks. In considering the events of the week we think it very necessary that the position of the military at the time should be borne in mind and their conduct should be viewed in the light of the abnormal circumstances then prevailing.

We now proceed to describe in order of time the events into which we have been directed to enquire.

Mr Sheehy Skeffington was the first of the three individuals to be arrested: his arrest had no connection with the arrest of Mr Dickson and Mr McIntyre, which occurred some three hours later.

Mr Francis Sheehy Skeffington was a well-known figure in Dublin, and shortly before 8 p.m. on 25th April he was walking from the city in the direction of his home, which was situated at 11, Grosvenor Place, Rathmines. His way led over Portobello Bridge, and about 350 yards further on he would have passed the turning which leads to the main entrance of Portobello Barracks.

It was conceded on all hands before us that Mr Sheehy Skeffington had no connection with the rebellion; his views were opposed to the use of physical force; and it appears that he had been engaged that afternoon in making some public appeal to prevent looting and the like. Mrs Sheehy Skeffington gave evidence of this fact, and her evidence is confirmed by a document which was found on him when he was searched and which contained a form of membership of a proposed civic organisation to check looting. As he approached Portobello Bridge he was followed by a crowd, some of the members of which were shouting out his name.

It was about dusk and the disturbances had now continued for some thirty hours. A young officer named Lieutenant M. C. Morris, who was attached to the 3rd Battalion of the Royal Irish Rifles at Portobello Barracks, had taken up duty an hour before in command of a picket at Portobello Bridge, occupying premises at the corner known as Davy's Public House. His orders were to do his utmost to avoid conflict but to keep the roadway clear as far as possible. Lieutenant Morris heard people in the street shouting out Mr Sheehy Skeffington's name, and he determined to detain him and send him to the barracks. Lieutenant Morris did not himself leave his post for many hours afterwards. He sent Mr Sheehy Skeffington under an escort of two men to the barracks.

We consider that there is no good ground of complaint against the action of Lieutenant Morris in causing Mr Sheehy Skeffington to be detained and sent to barracks. He told us that he had taken the same course with one or two others who seemed likely to cause a crowd to congregate; his picket had been fired at from time to time from houses close by; there was no police force in the streets; and it was obviously better to require pedestrians who appeared to be attracting notice to go to the barracks rather than run the risk of altercations in the roadway. No charge was made against Mr Sheehy Skeffington and he went quite willingly. Many other civilians against whom no charge was made were sent, in the course of the disturbances, to the barracks in similar circumstances, and the fact that they were innocent of all complicity in the rebellion does not necessarily imply that their temporary detention cannot be explained or justified. The really important matter in such cases is not the fact of detention but the subsequent treatment of the individuals detained.

On arrival at the barracks Mr Sheehy Skeffington was taken to the main guard-room; three young officers, named Dobbin, Tooley and Alexander Wilson, were sharing duty there, Mr Dobbin being the senior of the three. Mr Dobbin was only eighteen years of age, having left school in the previous year, and he had held his Commission only a few months; he had at that time seen nothing of fighting. He and the other two second lieutenants arranged among themselves spells of duty, and it was not clearly established before us which of them was in actual charge when Mr Sheehy Skeffington was brought in. Sergeant Maxwell, who was in the guard-room, was ordered to take Mr Sheehy Skeffington across to the orderly room to be interrogated, and he was there interviewed by the Adjutant of the Battalion, Lieutenant Morgan, who is an officer of experience. Evidence as to this interrogation is not quite precise or consistent, but the witnesses agreed that Mr Sheehy Skeffington stated that he was not a Sinn Feiner, but that he was in favour of passive resistance and opposed to militarism. Since there was no charge of any sort against Mr Sheehy Skeffington, Lieutenant Morgan thought it best to communicate by telephone with the Garrison Adjutant for instructions as to whether Mr Sheehy Skeffington should be further detained or not. Orders having been received that he should be detained for further inquiries, he was brought back to the guard-room.

Mr Sheehy Skeffington was searched by Captain Bowen-Colthurst. This gentleman was an officer of 16 years' service. He belonged to the Royal Irish Rifles, and had considerable experience of warfare. He had been with his battalion of the regiment at the front when he was seriously wounded and invalided home. At the time of the Dublin disturbances he was attached to the 3rd Battalion at Portobello Barracks. Having searched Mr Sheehy Skeffington, Captain Bowen-Colthurst at about 9 p.m. handed over to the Adjutant what he had found upon him. The Adjutant made copies of these documents and produced them before us; they were few in number, and none of them had anything to do with the disturbances save the document already referred to, which was a draft form of membership for a civic guard. There was nothing of an incriminatory nature found on Mr Sheehy Skeffington. When we come to deal with the cases of Mr Dickson and Mr McIntyre, it will again be seen that nothing of consequence was found upon them, and the absence of compromising documents in all three cases is, in the light of a report subsequently made by Captain Bowen-Colthurst, a fact of considerable importance.

Later, on the same evening, Captain Bowen-Colthurst went out of the barracks in command of a party under orders to enter and occupy premises at the corner of Camden Street and Harrington Street, occupied by Mr James Kelly for the purposes of his tobacco business. Mr Kelly is an Alderman of the City and a Justice of the Peace, and had recently held the office of High Sheriff of the City. There is no question that the suspicion entertained against Mr Kelly's loyalty was due to a misunderstanding, and that Mr Kelly was, in fact, quite innocent of any connection with the outbreak. Mr Kelly's premises are some 300 yards on the city side of Portobello Bridge, and the route for Captain Bowen-Colthurst's party therefore lay from the main gate of the barracks along the lane leading into the Rathmines Road, and then along the Rathmines Road over Portobello Bridge past Davy's Public House.

Captain Bowen-Colthurst adopted the extraordinary, and indeed almost meaningless, course of taking Mr Sheehy Skeffington with him as a "hostage". He had no right to take Mr Sheehy Skeffington out of the custody of the guard for this or any other purpose, and he asked no one's leave to do so. Captain Bowen-Colthurst's party consisted of a junior officer (Second Lieutenant Leslie Wilson) and about forty men. Before they left the barracks Mr Sheehy Skeffington's hands were tied behind his back and Captain Bowen-Colthurst called upon him to say his prayers. Upon Mr Sheehy Skeffington refusing to do so Captain Bowen-Colthurst ordered the men of his party to take their hats off and himself uttered a prayer, the words of it, according to Lieutenant Wilson's evidence, being: "O Lord God, if it shall please thee to take away the life of this man forgive him for Christ's sake."

The party proceeded from the main gate of the barracks to the turning into the Rathmines Road, where a shooting incident occurred which we thought it right to investigate since Mr Sheehy Skeffington was present and since it was suggested (though not proved) that it might have led to some protest on his part, or might have had some bearing upon his subsequent treatment. We find it impossible to reconcile all the testimony given on this matter, but it was established that a youth named Coade with a friend named Laurence Byrne were in the Rathmines Road when Captain Bowen-Colthurst's party came by. Captain Bowen-Colthurst asked what business they had to be in the road at that hour and warned them that martial law had been proclaimed. The evidence as to what next happened is not consistent, but there is no suggestion that either of the young men showed any violence, and it was clearly established before us that Captain Bowen-Colthurst shot young Coade, who fell mortally wounded and was subsequently taken by an ambulance to the hospital in the barracks. Lieutenant Leslie Wilson testified that Captain Bowen-Colthurst fired with a rifle, but two civilian witnesses—whose good faith there is no reason to doubt—asserted positively that they saw Captain Bowen-Colthurst (whose identity was unmistakable, since he is a man of exceptional stature) brandish and fire a revolver. There was admittedly other firing as Captain Bowen-Colthurst's party marched down the road, which Lieutenant Leslie Wilson told us was for the purpose of securing that people at the windows should keep indoors. The evidence of the different witnesses can only be reconciled by inferring that more than one case of shooting occurred during the progress of Captain Bowen-Colthurst's party.

None of the evidence offered to us afforded any justification for the shooting of Coade; it is, of course, a delusion to suppose that a proclamation of martial law confers upon an officer any right to take human life in circumstances where this would have been unjustifiable without such a proclamation, and this delusion in the present case had tragic consequences.

On reaching Portobello Bridge Captain Bowen-Colthurst divided his party into two and left half of it in the charge of Lieutenant Leslie Wilson, while going forward with the rest to attack Alderman Kelly's shop; he also left Mr Sheehy Skeffington at the bridge, giving Lieutenant Leslie Wilson orders that, if he (Captain Bowen-Colthurst) and his men were "knocked out", Lieutenant Leslie Wilson was to take command, and if they were fired upon Lieutenant Wilson was to shoot Mr Sheehy Skeffington.

The advance party then went on its way and was absent about twenty minutes; they threw a bomb into Alderman Kelly's shop and met with no resistance there. Alderman Kelly was absent; Mr McIntyre, who was a friend of Alderman Kelly, had been on the premises some time and Mr Dickson, who lived close by, took refuge there when he heard the soldiers firing as they approached. Miss Kelly, who is a sister of Alderman Kelly, gave us a detailed account of the raid on her brother's premises; it is evident from her account that Captain Bowen-Colthurst was in a state of great excitement. Dickson and McIntyre, together with two other men who were shortly afterwards released, were taken into custody, and Captain Bowen-Colthurst returned to barracks with them, picking up Mr Sheehy Skeffington and the other section of his party on the way.

Meanwhile, the news of Mr Sheehy Skeffington having been taken out of barracks reached the ears of the Adjutant, who fixed the time when he heard this from Sergeant Maxwell at about 10.20 p.m. The Adjutant saw Lieutenant Dobbin and asked him for a written report; this document was produced, and runs as follows:

> *25th April*, 11.10 p.m.
>
> An armed party under Captain J. C. Bowen-Colthurst has just passed through my guard, demanding and taking with him the last captured prisoner, Sheehy Skeffington.

It is important to observe that the terms of this document, while they show that Lieutenant Dobbin realised that the prisoners were in his custody and under his control, record a "demand" made upon him by an officer of superior rank and vastly greater experience. The report does not state that Captain Bowen-Colthurst was taking out Mr Sheehy Skeffington as a "hostage", and both the Adjutant and Lieutenant Dobbin assured us that they were ignorant of Captain Bowen-Colthurst's object.

When Captain Bowen-Colthurst returned to barracks he made a verbal report in the presence of the Adjutant to Major Rosborough in the course of which, according to the Adjutant, he mentioned that he had taken Mr Sheehy Skeffington with him and had arrested Dickson and McIntyre. The Adjutant was unable to give us a fuller account of the interview and he had no recollection of any reprimand being administered to Captain Bowen-Colthurst. Major Rosborough himself had no recollection of the interview at all, and explained that he was working at great pressure and under extreme anxiety and that whatever Captain Bowen-Colthurst said it never conveyed to his mind that Mr Sheehy Skeffington had been taken out in the way and for the purpose described. Nothing was said as to the shooting of Coade.

We are satisfied that the seriousness of the irregularity committed by Captain Bowen-Colthurst in his treatment of Mr Sheehy Skeffington on this Tuesday night was not fully realised by those under whose commands he was supposed to be acting. Whether from the lateness of the hour or from the strain and anxiety caused by events outside the barracks and the apprehension of even graver trouble, this officer was not effectively reprimanded, and the civilians detained under the main guard were not rendered more secure, with the result that Captain Bowen-Colthurst was at liberty the next morning again to override or disregard the officer of the guard, and to deal with civilian prisoners as he pleased.

Mr Dickson and Mr McIntyre were searched but nothing material was found on them. They spent the night in the detention room along with some other civilians. Mr Sheehy Skeffington, as being of a superior social position, was put into a separate cell and was made as comfortable as possible.

Mr Dickson was the editor of a paper called *The Eye-Opener*, and Mr McIntyre was the editor of

another paper known as *The Searchlight*. So far as there
was any evidence at all on the point before us, it
appears that the only reason for arresting either of
these men was the circumstance that they were found
on Alderman Kelly's premises, and, as we have already
stated, the suspicion entertained against this gentleman was without any foundation. Mr Dickson was a
Scotsman, and deformed. Neither he nor Mr
McIntyre had any connection with the Sinn Fein
movement.

On Wednesday morning, 26th April, the officers
in charge of the main guard were the same as on the
previous evening—namely, Lieutenants Dobbin,
Tooley, and Alexander Wilson. The sergeant of the
guard was Sergeant John W. Aldridge, then of the 10th
Royal Dublin Fusiliers. Sergeant Aldridge was on
leave at the commencement of the rebellion and on
returning to Dublin reported himself (like many
other soldiers at this time) at the nearest barracks; he
was in consequence new to his surroundings at
Portobello and the officers at the barracks were not
known to him by sight. He mounted guard at 9 a.m.
on Wednesday morning.

Shortly after 10 a.m. Captain Bowen-Colthurst
came to the guard room. He appears on his first
arrival to have entirely ignored Lieutenant Dobbin,
who was standing in the barrack square near to the
guard room entrance, and having passed into the guard
room itself to have given his orders direct to the
sergeant. These orders were to the effect that he
required the three prisoners, Skeffington, Dickson,

and McIntyre, in the yard for the purpose of speaking to them. The yard in question is within the guard room block of buildings, being reached by a short passage from the guard room. It comprises a space less than 40 ft in length and some 15 ft in width and is surrounded by high brick walls.

Sergeant Aldridge had not seen Captain Bowen-Colthurst before and was not aware of what position he occupied in the barracks save that his uniform showed him to be a captain. Owing to the sergeant having mounted guard only an hour previously he did not know who were the officers of the guard, and there was consequently nothing which appeared to him to be unusual in Captain Bowen-Colthurst entering the guard room and giving orders. The orders were complied with. Mr Sheehy Skeffington was called from his cell and Messrs. Dickson and McIntyre from the detention room, and all three were ordered out into the yard which was but a few paces away.

During the few moments that were occupied by the calling out of the three prisoners, Captain Bowen-Colthurst stepped out of the guard room to the spot where Lieutenant Dobbin was still standing and informed that officer that he was taking the three prisoners out for the purpose of shooting them, as he thought "it was the best thing to do". Lieutenant Dobbin's recollection is not clear as to whether the three men were mentioned by name, but there is no doubt that their number and the purpose for which Captain Bowen-Colthurst was taking them out were distinctly conveyed to his mind. Captain Bowen-Colthurst immediately re-entered the guard room, while Lieutenant Dobbin called to Lieutenant Alexander Wilson who was near-by and dispatched him with an urgent message to the Adjutant. Lieutenant Wilson had his bicycle with him; he mounted it and rode off to the orderly room in which the Adjutant was working and which is some 500 yards distant from the guard room.

Lieutenant Wilson's recollection of these vital incidents has varied from time to time, but we think there is no reason to question the sincerity of this witness in ultimately arriving at a conclusion as to what took place differing materially from his earlier impressions. Even so, his recollection of the message he delivered does not altogether agree with the Adjutant's memory on the point: the latter's version is corroborated by the evidence of Sergeant Campbell.

Lieutenant Dobbin's own statement is that he told Lieutenant Wilson to inform the Adjutant that Captain Bowen-Colthurst was taking the prisoners out of the guard room. He does not recollect stating in the message for what purpose they were being taken out. We think it probable that Captain Bowen-Colthurst's purpose was present to the mind of Lieutenant Wilson when he conveyed the message, but we are satisfied that the message itself as received by the Adjutant contained no mention of the fact that the prisoners were about to be shot. The impression made on the Adjutant's mind by the receipt of the message was that Captain Bowen-Colthurst was engaged in repeating his irregular proceedings of the evening before, and the message he returned by Lieutenant Wilson was that as Major Rosborough was out, that he (the Adjutant) could give no authority for any prisoners to be taken out of the guard room, and that in taking them out Captain Bowen-Colthurst would be acting on his own responsibility. Lieutenant Wilson returned with this message on his bicycle, and, while he was giving it to Lieutenant Dobbin just outside the guard room, the shots of the fatal volley rang out from the adjoining yard.

When Captain Bowen-Colthurst returned into the guard room after his brief statement to Lieutenant Dobbin he ordered some of the guard with their rifles out into the yard, where the three prisoners had preceded them. All the men on duty had their magazines already filled, and seven of the guard, who appear to have been merely those that happened at the moment to be nearest the yard passage, accompanied by Sergeant Aldridge, followed Captain Bowen-Colthurst out into the yard. What then occurred took place so rapidly that we have little doubt that none of the three victims realised that they were about to meet their death. We are confirmed in this view by the fact that all the witnesses, including civilian prisoners in the detention room, to whom everything that took place in the yard was audible, agree in stating that no sound was uttered by any of the three.

While the soldiers were entering the yard Captain Bowen-Colthurst ordered the three prisoners to walk to the wall at the other end, a distance, as we have stated, of only a few yards. As they were doing this the seven soldiers, entering the yard, fell into line along the wall adjoining the entrance, and immediately received from Captain Colthurst the order to fire upon the three prisoners who had then just turned to face them. All three fell as a result of the volley. Captain Bowen-Colthurst left the yard, and the firing party began to file out.

Immediately upon hearing the volley, Lieutenant Dobbin (who was engaged in receiving the Adjutant's message outside) hastened through the guard room and entered the yard. On looking at the bodies he saw a movement in one of Mr Sheehy Skeffington's legs which gave him the impression that life was not yet extinct, and he exclaimed to Sergeant Aldridge, who was still in the yard, "Sergeant, that man is not dead." It is Sergeant Aldridge's impression (and we are inclined to accept the evidence of this witness, who was both experienced and candid) that death had, nevertheless, been instantaneous in all three cases, and that what Lieutenant Dobbin saw was a muscular contraction of the unfortunate gentleman's limb. As a result, however, of what he saw, Lieutenant Dobbin dispatched one of the other officers of the guard, Lieutenant Tooley, to the orderly room to report and obtain instructions. At, or in the neighbourhood of, the orderly room Lieutenant Tooley met Captain Bowen-Colthurst, and received from him the order to "fire again". Lieutenant Tooley returned with this message, and thereupon four soldiers of the guard (not all members of the first firing party) were ordered into the yard by Lieutenant Dobbin, and upon his directions fired a second volley into the body of Mr Sheehy Skeffington.

Certain civilian witnesses who were in the detention room during the course of these events spoke to having heard a shot, or volley, in addition to, and separated by a distinct interval of time from, the two volleys spoken of by the military. If their evidence be correct (and there is no reason to doubt their good faith) this third shot, or volley, was heard at a moment antecedent to Messrs. Dickson and McIntyre reaching the yard, and the question was raised by those appearing for the relatives of Mr Sheehy Skeffington whether the latter had not been shot separately from the other two prisoners. We are quite satisfied on the evidence as a whole that the three prisoners were shot together in the way we have described, and that the earlier report by those in the detention room had no connection with any shooting in the yard. It may perhaps be explained by the accidental discharge of a rifle near the guard room, which was the impression conveyed to at least one of those in the detention room.

It should be clearly understood that the events we have been recording, from the arrival of Captain Bowen-Colthurst at the guard room, occupied but a very few minutes. The guard room, detention room, detention cells, and yard all closely adjoin one another in the same block, and a very few steps suffice to take a person from one into another.

Not long after the shooting had taken place, and before 10.30 a.m., Captain Bowen-Colthurst reported verbally to the Adjutant at the orderly room that he had shot Mr Sheehy Skeffington and the editors of the *Eye-Opener* and *The Searchlight*. Either then or later, he gave as his reason for so doing the fear that they would escape or might be rescued by armed force. There was no foundation whatever for any apprehension as to the escape of these prisoners, and no sane person who honestly entertained such a possibility as a rescue would have seen in it any ground for distinction between these three prisoners and the other detained persons. At or about the same time, Captain Bowen-Colthurst verbally reported his action to Major Rosborough, adding that he had shot the three prisoners on his own responsibility and that he possibly might be hanged for it. Major Rosborough told him to make his report in writing, and instructed the Adjutant to report the matter to the Garrison Adjutant at Dublin Castle.

Lieutenant Morgan, after going over to the guard room and seeing the three bodies carried out, telephoned, in accordance with his instructions from Major Rosborough, a report of the circumstances, as far as they were then known to him, to the Garrison Adjutant (Captain Burton). A telephonic report on other matters was about this time being made to Headquarters, Irish Command, and, in view of the seriousness of the occurrence, the Adjutant, under Major Rosborough's directions, did not confine himself to the usual channel, but also made a direct communication by telephone to Headquarters, Irish Command. Major Rosborough had, in the meanwhile, given directions that Captain Bowen-Colthurst should not be detailed for duty outside the barracks. No further action was taken as regards Captain Bowen-Colthurst until 6th May, when orders were received from the superior military authorities to place Captain Bowen-Colthurst under open arrest. Major Rosborough's directions as to his duties do not seem to have placed any effective check upon his movements in the meantime.

Later in the day, Lieutenant Morgan telephoned again to the Garrison Adjutant in order to ask for directions as to the disposal of the bodies (which were lying in the mortuary), and was ordered to bury them in the barrack yard that evening. Lieutenant Morgan, accordingly, after consultation with the Medical Officer, Major Balch, and also the Engineer Officer, had the bodies wrapped up in sheets and buried in the barrack square. It should be remembered that, in the then state of the city, coffins were difficult, if not impossible, to secure, and the same mode of burial had to be adopted in the case of soldiers whose bodies were brought into the barracks. We are satisfied that Lieutenant Morgan carried out his duties in connection with the burial as decorously and reverently as was possible in the circumstances at the time. He ascertained that all three of the deceased were Roman Catholics and the religious rites were carried out by Father O'Loughlin, the Roman Catholic chaplain of the barracks. At a later date, at the request of the relatives and by permission of Sir John Maxwell (who had arrived in Ireland some days after these shootings), the bodies of all three men were exhumed and re-interred in consecrated ground. Mr Sheehy Skeffington, Senior, was present at the exhumation of his son's body.

From time to time during the course of Wednesday, 26th April, Major Rosborough pressed Captain Bowen-Colthurst for the written report which he had directed him to make; it was ultimately received at a late hour in the afternoon, and, so far as it is material to our inquiry, it reads as follows:

Sir,

I have to report for your information that yesterday evening, about 11 p.m., according to your orders, I proceeded with a party of 25 men to Kelly's tobacco shop in Harcourt Road.

Some shots were fired at them, but whether from this shop or not I cannot say. Two men were seen standing in conversation outside the shop, who at once bolted inside. An entrance was effected and four men were made prisoners, two of these were subsequently released, and two men were detained. The two men detained were McIntyre, editor of *The Searchlight*, and Dickson, editor of the *Eye-Opener*.

Sniping was going on, and I lodged the two men detained in the Portobello guard room. I may add that I was informed that all of the tobacco had previously been removed. This morning at about 9 a.m. I proceeded to the guard room to examine these two men, and I sent for a man called Skeffington, who was also detained.

I had been busy on the previous evening up to about 3 a.m. examining documents found on these three men, and I recognised from these documents that these 3 men were all very dangerous characters. I, therefore, sent for an armed guard of six men and ordered them to load their rifles and keep their eyes on the prisoners. The guard room was full of men and was not a suitable place, in my opinion, in which to examine prisoners. I ordered, therefore, the 3 prisoners to go into the small courtyard of the guard room. I regret now that I did not have these three men handcuffed and surrounded, as the yard was a place from which they might have escaped. When I ordered these three men into the yard I did not, however, know this. The guard was some little distance from the prisoners, and as I considered that there was a reasonable chance of the prisoners making their escape; and knowing the three prisoners (from the correspondence captured on them the previous evening) to be dangerous characters, I called upon the guard to fire upon them, which they did with effect, the 3 men being killed. The documents found on these 3 men have been forwarded to the orderly room.

It is to be noted that, although this report purports to give an account of the raid on Alderman Kelly's tobacco shop, no mention is made of Mr Sheehy Skeffington having been taken out as a "hostage" on that occasion, or of the shooting of the young man Coade. The account of the events which took place on Wednesday morning is entirely untrue. Captain Bowen-Colthurst's object in going to the guard room was not to examine the prisoners, but, as he stated to Lieutenant Dobbin at the time, to have them shot. The armed guard was not ordered out for the purpose of preventing the prisoners' escape, but for the purpose of shooting them. There was no possibility of the prisoners making their escape from the yard, a fact which is obvious to anyone who has seen it. No documents or correspondence whatever were found on the prisoners which showed them to be "dangerous characters"; and any documents found on them could be thoroughly examined in a few minutes.

At a later date, and after he had been placed under arrest, viz., on 9th May, 1916, Captain Bowen-Colthurst forwarded a further report addressed to the Officer Commanding 3rd Battalion of the Royal Irish Rifles. This report reads as follows:

> Sir,
>
> In accordance with instructions, I have the honour to forward for your information a more detailed account of the circumstances connected with the shooting of 3 rebels in Portobello Barracks, Dublin.
>
> On Tuesday evening, 25th ultimo, I was officially informed that martial law was declared in Dublin. There were 3 leaders of the rebels in the guard room in Portobello Barracks. The guard room was not safe for these desperate men to be confined in, their rescue from outside would be very easy.

On Tuesday and up to Wednesday morning
rumours of massacres of police and soldiers from all
parts of Dublin were being constantly sent to me
from different sources. Among others the rumour
reached me that 600 German prisoners at Oldcastle
had been released and armed and were marching on
Dublin. I also heard that the rebels in the city had
opened up depôts for the supply and issue of arms,
and that a large force of rebels intended to attack
Portobello Barracks, which was held only by a few
troops, many of whom were recruits ignorant as to
how to use their rifles, and a number of the others
were soldiers and sailors who had taken refuge in the
barracks. We had also in the barracks a considerable
number of officers and men who had been wounded
by the rebels and whose protection was a source of
great concern to me. I believed that it was known
that these leaders were confined in the barracks and
that possibly the proposed attack on the barracks was
with a view to their release. Rumours of risings all
over Ireland and of a large German-American and
Irish-American landing in Galway were prevalent. I
had no knowledge of any reinforcements arriving
from England, and did not believe it possible for
troops from England to arrive in time to prevent a
general massacre. I knew of the sedition which had
been preached in Ireland for years past and of the
popular sympathy with rebellion. I knew also that
men on leave home from the trenches, although
unarmed, had been shot down like dogs in the streets
of their own city, simply because they were in khaki,

and I had also heard that wounded soldiers home for convalescence had been shot down also. On the Wednesday morning the 26th April all this was in my mind. I was very much exhausted and unstrung after practically a sleepless night, and I took the gloomiest view of the situation and felt that only desperate measures would save the situation. When I saw the position described in my previous report I felt I must act quickly, and believing I had the power under martial law, I felt, under the circumstances, that it was clearly my duty to have the three ring-leaders shot. It was a terrible ordeal for me, but I nerved myself to carry out what was for me at the time a terrible duty.

So far as this second report repeats the previous explanation as to the shooting having taken place with the object of preventing escape or rescue, the observations we have already made on this point apply to it. With the reference to martial law and the powers which this officer claimed to exercise under it, we deal in a later paragraph of this report. He is at present, as was proved to our satisfaction, confined in Broadmoor Criminal Lunatic Asylum consequent upon the sentence of a Court Martial (which found him guilty of murder but insane at the time of committing the crime), and we have therefore felt ourselves debarred from taking his evidence.

The disturbances continued throughout the week, and on Friday (28th April) Mrs Sheehy Skeffington, who had last seen her husband in Westmoreland Street on the previous Tuesday afternoon, was still without definite information as to what had happened to him. As a result of alarming rumours about him which reached her from various sources her two sisters, Mrs Culhane and Mrs Kettle, on the morning of Friday, went to the police station at Rathmines to make enquiries. The police had no information to give, but suggested that the two ladies might enquire at Portobello Barracks, where they accordingly went.

To appreciate what followed it is necessary to say a word as to Mrs Sheehy Skeffington and her two sisters. They are the daughters of Mr David Sheehy, M.P. Their brother, Lieutenant Sheehy, of the Dublin Fusiliers, was engaged in the fighting which was still taking place in Dublin. The husband of Mrs Culhane, then recently deceased, had been a highly placed and responsible official in the Irish Courts of Justice, while Mrs Kettle's husband, Lieutenant T.M. Kettle (who since our sittings has gallantly given his life for his country in France) was with his battalion. In such circumstances Mrs Sheehy Skeffington not unreasonably expected that whatever fate had overtaken her own husband, her two sisters would at least be treated with candour and consideration at the barracks, and would be able to obtain such information as was available about their brother-in-law.

Mrs Kettle and her sister arrived at the barracks at about 1 p.m., and after some slight delay were admitted past the first and second gates. A junior officer, Lieutenant Beattie, came up to enquire as to their business. This gentleman was not called before us, but as regards both this and the subsequent events to which Mrs Kettle and Mrs Sheehy Skeffington speak, we were expressly informed by those representing the military authorities, that the accuracy of the evidence given by these ladies was not called in question. Indeed, Lieutenant Beattie was present at the Inquiry, and we were told that his evidence was unnecessary since it would not controvert what Mrs Kettle stated.

Mrs Kettle and her sister thought it well to commence their enquiries by asking in the first place as to their brother, Lieutenant Sheehy. To this they received a courteous reply. They then asked as to their brother-in-law, Mr Sheehy Skeffington, whereupon the young officer with whom they were conversing betrayed some confusion, asked them to excuse him, and went away to consult with some other officers. On returning he informed the two ladies that he regretted that he would have to place them under arrest, giving as his reason that they were Sinn Feiners and had been seen speaking to Sinn Feiners. Mrs Kettle and her sister pointed out the absurdity of the allegation, and referred to the position of Lieutenant Kettle and of the late Mr Culhane; they were, however, placed in charge of some soldiers and marched across the barrack square to the orderly room, outside which they remained standing, surrounded by soldiers, while a consultation of officers appears to have taken place within. After some minutes Captain Bowen-Colthurst emerged from the guard room and questioned them. They repeated their enquiries as to Lieutenant Sheehy and as to Mr Sheehy Skeffington. Captain Colthurst, in reply to the latter enquiry, said, "I know nothing whatever about Mr Sheehy Skeffington." Mrs Culhane referred to some of the rumours which had reached them, and Lieutenant Beattie, who was the only other officer actually present at this interview, made some remark to Captain Bowen-Colthurst in an undertone. Captain Bowen-Colthurst then said, "I have no information concerning Mr Skeffington that is available, and the sooner you leave the barracks the better." There was then an order given to have the ladies conducted back, and, by Captain Bowen-Colthurst's direction, they were forbidden to speak to one another. The guard was dismissed at the gate and the two ladies were conducted to the tramway line by Lieutenant Beattie.

It is obvious to us that throughout the incidents recorded in the last paragraph Lieutenant Beattie acted under superior orders, and the evidence satisfied us that the part he was called upon to play was extremely distasteful to him.

About 4 p.m. on the afternoon of Friday, after receiving her sisters' report of what had just taken place in the barracks, Mrs Sheehy Skeffington got into touch with the father of the young man Coade to whose death we have referred. Father O'Loughlin, the Chaplain of the barracks whom we have already mentioned, knew young Coade as a member of the religious sodality of which he (Father O'Loughlin) was spiritual director, and at a meeting of which Coade had been present on the night he met his death. The father of Coade was informed of his son's fate by Father O'Loughlin and was permitted to visit the dead body in the mortuary at the barracks. Here the unfortunate man saw the body of Mr Sheehy Skeffington laid out beside that of his son, a fact which on Friday afternoon he communicated to Mrs Sheehy Skeffington. Mrs Sheehy Skeffington, on Mr Coade's suggestion, at once sought out Father O'Loughlin and besought him for particulars as to her husband. She was told that he was dead and already buried.

At 7 p.m. on this same Friday evening Mrs Sheehy Skeffington was putting her little son, aged seven, to bed, when a body of soldiers from Portobello Barracks headed by Captain Bowen-Colthurst and Colonel Allett (an officer of advanced years who had returned to service after the outbreak of the war and who was killed during the later stages of the rebellion) arrived at the house. Mrs Sheehy Skeffington was alone in the house save for her boy and a young maid-servant. Before any attempt was made to obtain an entrance into the house a volley was fired through the windows. A body of soldiers with fixed bayonets under Captain Bowen-Colthurst then burst in through the front door. No request for the door to be opened was made nor was any time given to those in the house to open it. Mrs Skeffington and her boy had bayonets pointed at them and were ordered to hold their hands above their heads. They were then, by orders of Captain Bowen-Colthurst, placed in the front room together with the maid and kept guarded while the house was searched.

All the rooms in the house were thoroughly ransacked and a considerable quantity of books and papers were wrapped up in the household linen, placed in a passing motor car, and taken away. Mrs Sheehy Skeffington has been herself a teacher of foreign languages while Mr Sheehy Skeffington was at the time the editor of a paper known as *The Irish Citizen,* and a large part of the material removed seems to have consisted of text-books both in German and other languages, as well as political papers and pamphlets belonging to Mr Sheehy Skeffington. The search lasted until a quarter past ten when the soldiers departed; Mrs Sheehy Skeffington together with her boy and maid-servant remained under arrest up to that hour.

On Monday, 1st May, Mrs Sheehy Skeffington's house was again visited by soldiers between 11 a.m. and 1 p.m., but Captain Bowen-Colthurst had nothing to do with this second visit. Neither Mrs Skeffington nor her boy were in the house at the time, the only occupant being a temporary maid-servant, Margaret Farrelly by name, a girl aged nineteen or twenty. Mrs Skeffington's previous servant had been terrified by her experiences on the Friday and had left, and the maid Farrelly had been obtained from one of Mrs Skeffington's sisters. Sergeant Claxton told us that he received a message, transmitted through the police, that an unknown person had been seen entering the house. Consequently, two soldiers in charge of this sergeant went there and the maid-servant was arrested and taken to Rathmines

Police Station. She was detained until the following Saturday when by the efforts of Mrs Skeffington's sisters her release was effected. Nothing else appears to have taken place on the occasion of this visit to the house.

Mr Dickson's house at 12, Harrington Street was visited by a military search-party during the course of Wednesday, 26th April, and a bag with some documents in it was taken away and left temporarily with the picket which was still in occupation of Alderman Kelly's tobacco shop near by. It was suggested before us that this was done with the object of attaching suspicion to Alderman Kelly, but we are satisfied that this was not the case and that the incident must be judged merely as an ineffectual attempt to obtain evidence which might justify or excuse the shooting which had already taken place at Portobello Barracks.

Before the outbreak of the rebellion in Dublin, much attention had been attracted to a printed pamphlet entitled "Secret Orders Issued to the Military". This pamphlet had been widely circulated with a view to creating the impression that its contents represented the text of confidential directions issued by the military authorities with the object of an attack upon the Sinn Fein organisation and its supporters. The document was a forgery from beginning to end, and the false representations it contained as to the orders actually issued, no doubt, played some part in precipitating the outbreak of the rebellion.

A copy of this document was produced before us with the following note attached to it in red ink and in the writing of Captain Bowen-Colthurst: "I certify that I found this document on the person of F. Sheehy Skeffington—J. W. Bowen-Colthurst, Captain RIR, Portobello Barracks, 25/4/16." Lieutenant Morgan, who took a careful copy of all the documents found on Mr Sheehy Skeffington on the night that he was arrested, satisfied us that this document was not among them, and, moreover, that it was not attached to Captain Bowen-Colthurst's report written on the day of the shooting. It is quite certain that Captain Bowen-Colthurst added this document, together with the above note appended to it, to those documents actually found on Mr Sheehy Skeffington at a later date than that which the note bears, and that the certificate endorsed upon it was untrue. The document itself was probably found by Captain Bowen-Colthurst at Mr Sheehy Skeffington's house at the search after his death, and the false certificate was added later. It was conceded before us that some copy of the printed document could have hardly failed to have come into the hands of any Dublin journalist. We think it right to state explicitly that no other person is in any way implicated in this misrepresentation, and the matter is only of importance as a further instance of the endeavours made by Captain Bowen-Colthurst, after the event, to excuse his action.

As a result of a communication to the military authorities in London, made by Major Sir Francis Vane (one of many officers who had reported at Portobello Barracks at the commencement of the outbreak), Captain Bowen-Colthurst was placed under "open" arrest upon 6th May, and subsequently on 11th May under "close" arrest. Major Sir Francis Vane was not an officer of the regiment stationed at the barracks and had no responsibility for any of the events we have described. On the 6th and 7th of June, Captain Bowen-Colthurst was tried by court-martial in Dublin for the murder of the three men and was found guilty but insane.

We have thought it formed no part of our duty to conduct any inquiry of our own into the state of Captain Bowen-Colthurst's mind at the time he committed the offence of which he has already been found guilty or to hear any evidence upon the point. The court-martial pronounced on this matter, and its conclusion is on record. Apart from the defence of insanity, there can be no excuse or palliation for his conduct from first to last, a state of things which was frankly recognised by those who appeared before us on behalf of the military authorities.

We have now set out all the relevant facts and circumstances as they appear to us and as we were able to ascertain them. We desire to add the following general observations which those facts and circumstances suggest to us:

(1) In order to form any fair judgment of the conduct of the officers and men at Portobello Barracks during Easter week, the very exceptional character of the circumstances in which they were placed must carefully be borne in mind. The garrison of the barracks, insufficient as

it was for the purpose of resisting any serious assault that might have been made, was reinforced by a medley of soldiers from different regiments, together with some sailors who had reported at the commencement of the week. The officers, too, came from different units and were in many cases unknown to one another. It is not to be wondered at that this state of things produced a considerable laxity of control and cohesion within the barracks. It was in such novel and disturbing conditions that the battalion stationed at the barracks found itself deprived of its Commanding Officer, Colonel McCammond, through his serious illness. Captain Bowen-Colthurst was the senior captain in the barracks, and, although not the equal in rank, was of longer standing and of greater experience in the Army than Major Rosborough. The latter officer, as well as the Adjutant, Lieutenant Morgan, were fully occupied with the many important duties to which the emergency had given rise. Messages of an alarming character were constantly being transmitted to them from outside, and the exercise of effective control over an officer in Captain Bowen-Colthurst's position was rendered doubly difficult. We are satisfied that the state of things which rendered Captain Bowen-Colthurst's conduct possible was largely caused by the unfortunate but inevitable absence of Colonel McCammond, the only officer in the barracks whom Captain Colthurst would not have considered himself at liberty to ignore. The officers in charge of the guard were young men who had recently left school, and, of necessity, were without military experience; and this fact, combined with Captain Colthurst's masterful character and superior rank, does much to excuse their failure to offer any effective opposition to his treatment of prisoners who were under their charge.

(2) No evidence as to the raid on Mrs Sheehy Skeffington's house on Friday evening, 28th April, was tendered to us on behalf of the military, save that Major Rosborough denied that he had given any orders for it—a statement which we accept. A large number of soldiers took part in the raid, and it is impossible to suppose that the facts as to it remained unknown to all not actually engaged in it, though we cannot believe that the methods employed were either authorised or approved. The discreditable character of the proceeding is intensified by the circumstance that a few hours before, when inquiries were made at the barracks on Mrs Sheehy Skeffington's behalf, information was refused by the officer responsible for her husband's death, who himself then headed the raid. We think it right to say that, in our opinion, it is a circumstance highly regrettable and most surprising that, after the events of Wednesday, Captain Bowen-Colthurst should have found himself free to act, in company with a body of soldiers, as he did on the following Friday.

(3) The effect, so far as the powers of military authorities are concerned, of a proclamation of martial law within the United Kingdom has often been expounded, but nevertheless, in the crisis which evokes such a proclamation, is not always remembered. Such a proclamation does not, in itself, confer upon officers or soldiers any new powers. It operates solely as a warning that the Government, acting through the military, is about to take such forcible and exceptional measures as may be necessary for the purpose of putting down insurrection and restoring order. As long as the measures are necessary, they might equally be taken without any proclamation at all. The measures that are taken can only be justified by the circumstances then existing and the practical necessities of the case. Yet Miss Kelly told us that when Captain Bowen-Colthurst entered her brother's premises he warned those present that "as martial law had been proclaimed" he could shoot them as he had shot someone in the street; Captain Bowen-Colthurst, in his second report on the shootings, claims to have acted under the belief that he was exercising powers conferred on him by martial law; and we heard from the young officer who was left with Mr Sheehy Skeffington at Portobello Bridge while Captain Bowen-Colthurst went forward, that he saw nothing "strange" in the order that he was to shoot Mr Sheehy Skeffington in the event of anything happening to Captain Bowen-Colthurst's party three

hundred yards off. The shooting of unarmed and unresisting civilians without trial constitutes the offence of murder, whether martial law has been proclaimed or not. We should have deemed it superfluous to point this out were it not that the failure to realise and apply this elementary principle seems to explain the free hand which Captain Bowen-Colthurst was not restrained from exercising throughout the period of crisis.

We desire to state that we have had every assistance from the military authorities in obtaining all the documents and evidence at their disposal which we required for the purposes of our inquiry, and that we are indebted to all who appeared before us for their help in elucidating the course of these lamentable events.

Finally, we desire to express our cordial appreciation of the valuable services rendered to us by our Secretary, Mr Harold L. Murphy, both during our sittings and in the preparation of this report.

All which we humbly submit and report for Your Majesty's gracious consideration.

29th September, 1916

JOHN SIMON
THOMAS F. MOLONY
DENIS S. HENRY
HAROLD L. MURPHY
Secretary

PART V

⚬⚬✖⚬⚬

CORRESPONDENCE

RELATING TO THE

PROPOSALS OF HIS MAJESTY'S GOVERNMENT FOR AN IRISH SETTLEMENT

1921

The General Election of 1918 saw a massive electoral swing in Ireland in favour of the Sinn Fein party. In 1919 Sinn Fein set up a republican government in Ireland, ignoring the British authorities completely. The Sinn Fein MPs refused to sit in the Westminster parliament, instead preferring to set up their own parliament, the Dale Eireann, in Dublin.

Eamon de Valera was one of the senior members of the Easter Rising who escaped execution in 1916, becoming leader of Sinn Fein in 1917. David Lloyd George was the British Prime Minister of the time with whom he was to negotiate.

The papers presented here were published by the British Government in anticipation of an Anglo-Irish Conference to be held in London in 1921. This conference was to lead to a new stage in the history of Anglo-Irish affairs, and indeed to a civil war in Ireland. They are included here as an indication of the public tone adopted by both parties at this time.

The Prime Minister's letter to Mr de Valera, outlining the proposals of the British Government for an Irish settlement
                                                    20th July 1921

The British Government are actuated by an earnest desire to end the unhappy divisions between Great Britain and Ireland which have produced so many conflicts in the past and which have once more shattered the peace and well-being of Ireland at the present time. They long with His Majesty the King, in the words of His Gracious Speech in Ireland last month, for a satisfactory solution of "those age-long Irish problems which for generations embarrassed our forefathers, as they now weigh heavily upon us"; and they wish to do their utmost to secure that "every man of Irish birth, whatever be his creed and wherever be his home, should work in loyal co-operation with the free communities on which the British Empire is based." They are convinced that the Irish people may find as worthy and as complete an expression of their political and spiritual ideals within the Empire as any of the numerous and varied nations united in allegiance to His Majesty's Throne; and they desire such a consummation, not only for the welfare of Great Britain, Ireland and the Empire as a whole, but also for the cause of peace and harmony throughout the world. There is no part of the world where Irishmen have made their home but suffers from our ancient feuds; no part of it but looks to this meeting between the British Government and the Irish leaders to resolve these feuds in a new understanding, honourable and satisfactory to all the peoples involved.

The free nations which compose the British Empire are drawn from many races, with different histories, traditions and ideals. In the Dominion of Canada, British and French have long forgotten the bitter conflicts which divided their ancestors. In South Africa the Transvaal Republic and the Orange Free State have joined with two British colonies to make a great self-governing union under His Majesty's sway. The British people cannot believe that where Canada and South Africa, with equal or even greater difficulties, have so signally succeeded, Ireland will fail; and they are determined that, so far as they themselves can assure it, nothing shall hinder Irish statesmen from joining together to build up an Irish State in free and willing co-operation with the other peoples of the Empire.

Moved by these considerations, the British Government invite Ireland to take her place in the great association of free nations over which His Majesty reigns. As earnest of their desire to obliterate old quarrels and to enable Ireland to face the future with her own strength and hope, they propose that Ireland shall assume forthwith the status of a Dominion, with all the powers and privileges set forth in this document. By the adoption of Dominion status it is understood that Ireland shall enjoy complete autonomy in taxation and finance; that she shall maintain her own courts of law and judges; that she shall maintain her own military forces for home defence, her own constabulary and her own police; that she shall take over the Irish postal services and all matters relating thereto, education, land, agriculture, mines and minerals, forestry, housing, labour, unemployment, transport, trade, public health, health insurance and the liquor traffic; and, in sum, that she shall exercise all those powers and privileges upon which the autonomy of the self-governing Dominions is based, subject only to the considerations set out in the ensuing paragraphs. Guaranteed in these liberties, which no foreign people can challenge without challenging the Empire as a whole, the Dominions hold each and severally by virtue of their

British fellowship a standing amongst the nations equivalent, not merely to their individual strength, but to the combined power and influence of all the nations of the Commonwealth. That guarantee, that fellowship, that freedom the whole Empire looks to Ireland to accept.

To this settlement the British Government are prepared to give immediate effect upon the following conditions, which are, in their opinion, vital to the welfare and safety of both Great Britain and Ireland, forming as they do the heart of the Commonwealth:

I. The common concern of Great Britain and Ireland in the defence of their interests by land and sea shall be mutually recognised. Great Britain lives by sea-borne food; her communications depend upon the freedom of the great sea routes. Ireland lies at Britain's side across the seaways north and south that link her with the sister nations of the Empire, the markets of the world and the vital sources of her food supply. In recognition of this fact, which nature has imposed and no statesmanship can change, it is essential that the Royal Navy alone should control the seas around Ireland and Great Britain, and that such rights and liberties should be accorded to it by the Irish State as are essential for naval purposes in the Irish harbours and on the Irish coasts.

II. In order that the movement towards the limitation of armaments which is now making progress in the world should in no way be hampered, it is stipulated that the Irish Territorial Force shall, within reasonable limits, conform in respect of numbers to the military establishments of the other parts of these islands.

III. The position of Ireland is also of great importance for the air services, both military and civil. The Royal Air Force will need facilities for all purposes that it serves, and Ireland will form an essential link in the development of air routes between the British Isles and the North American continent. It is therefore stipulated that Great Britain shall have all necessary facilities for the development of defence and of communications by air.

IV. Great Britain hopes that Ireland will, in due course and of her own free will, contribute in proportion to her wealth to the Regular Naval, Military and Air Forces of the Empire. It is further assumed that voluntary recruitment for these forces will be permitted throughout Ireland, particularly for those famous Irish regiments which have so long and so gallantly served His Majesty in all parts of the world.

V. While the Irish people shall enjoy complete autonomy in taxation and finance, it is essential to prevent a recurrence of ancient differences between the two islands, and in particular to avert the possibility of ruinous trade wars. With this object in view, the British and Irish Governments shall agree to impose no protective duties or other restrictions upon the flow of transport, trade and commerce between all parts of these islands.

VI. The Irish people shall agree to assume responsibility for a share of the present debt of the United Kingdom and of the liability for pensions arising out of the great war, the share, in default of agreement between the Governments concerned, to be determined by an independent arbitrator appointed from within His Majesty's dominions.

In accordance with these principles, the British Government propose that the conditions of settlement between Great Britain and Ireland shall be embodied in the form of a treaty, to which effect shall in due course be given by the British and Irish Parliaments. They look to such an instrument to obliterate old conflicts forthwith, to clear the way for a detailed settlement in full accordance with Irish conditions and needs, and thus to establish a new and happier relation between Irish patriotism and that wider community of aims and interests by which the unity of the whole Empire is freely sustained.

The form in which the settlement is to take effect will depend upon Ireland herself. It must allow for full recognition of the existing powers and privileges of the Parliament and Government of Northern Ireland, which cannot be abrogated except by their own consent. For their part, the British Government entertain an earnest hope that the necessity of harmonious co-operation amongst Irishmen of all classes and creeds will be recognised throughout Ireland, and they will welcome the day when by these means unity is achieved, but no such common action can be secured by force. Union came in Canada by the free consent of the provinces. So in Australia; so in South Africa. It will come in Ireland by no other way than consent. There can, in fact, be no settlement on terms involving, on the one side or the other, that bitter appeal to bloodshed and violence which all men of goodwill are longing to terminate. The British Government will undertake to give effect, so far as that depends on them, to any terms in this respect on which all Ireland unites. But in no conditions can they consent to any proposals which would kindle civil war in Ireland. Such a war would not touch Ireland alone, for partisans would flock to either side from Great Britain, the Empire and elsewhere with consequences more devastating to the welfare both of Ireland and the Empire than the conflict to which a truce has been called this month. Throughout the Empire there is a deep desire that the day of violence should pass and that a solution should be found, consonant with the highest ideals and interests of all parts of Ireland, which will enable her to co-operate as a willing partner in the British Commonwealth.

The British Government will therefore leave Irishmen themselves to determine by negotiations between them whether the new powers which the pact defines shall be taken over by Ireland as a whole and administered by a single Irish body, or taken over separately by Southern and Northern Ireland, with or without a joint authority to harmonise their common interests. They will willingly assist in the negotiation of such a settlement, if Irishmen should so desire.

By these proposals the British Government sincerely believe that they will have shattered the foundations of that ancient hatred and distrust which have disfigured our common history for centuries past. The future of Ireland within the Commonwealth is for the Irish people to shape.

In the foregoing proposals the British Government have attempted no more than the broad outline of a settlement. The details they leave for discussion when the Irish people have signified their acceptance of the principle of this pact.

D. LLOYD GEORGE
10, *Downing Street*, SW1

Reply from Mr de Valera to D. Lloyd George
(Official translation)

Mansion House, Dublin

Sir,   10*th August,* 1921

On the occasion of our last interview I gave it as my judgment that Dail Eireann could not, and that the Irish people would not, accept the proposals of your Government as set forth in the draft of the 20th July, which you had presented to me. Having consulted my colleagues, and with them given these proposals the most earnest consideration, I now confirm that judgment.

The outline given in the draft is self-contradictory; and "the principle of the pact" not easy to determine. To the extent that it implies a recognition of Ireland's separate nationhood and her right to self-determination we appreciate and accept it. But in the stipulations and express conditions concerning the matters that are vital the principle is strangely set aside and a claim advanced by your Government to an interference in our affairs and to a control which we cannot admit.

Ireland's right to choose for herself the path she shall take to realise her own destiny must be accepted as indefeasible. It is a right that has been maintained through centuries of oppression and at the cost of unparalleled sacrifice and untold suffering, and it will not be surrendered. We cannot propose to abrogate or impair it, nor can Britain or any other foreign State or group of States legitimately claim to interfere with its exercise in order to serve their own special interests.

The Irish people's belief is that the national destiny can best be realised in political detachment, free from imperialistic entanglements which they feel will involve enterprises out of harmony with the national character, prove destructive of their ideals, and be fruitful only of ruinous wars, crushing burdens, social discontent, and general unrest and unhappiness. Like the small States of Europe, they are prepared to hazard their independence on the basis of moral right, confident that as they would threaten no nation or people, they would in turn be free from aggression themselves. This is the policy they have declared for in plebiscite after plebiscite, and the degree to which any other line of policy deviates from it must be taken as a measure of the extent to which external pressure is operative and violence is being done to the wishes of the majority.

As for myself and my colleagues, it is our deep conviction that true friendship with England, which military coercion has frustrated for centuries, can be obtained most readily now through amicable but absolute separation. The fear, groundless though we believe it to be, that Irish territory may be used as the basis for an attack upon England's liberties can be met by reasonable guarantees not inconsistent with Irish sovereignty.

"Dominion status" for Ireland everyone who understands the conditions knows to be illusory. The freedom which the British Dominions enjoy is not so much the result of legal enactments or of treaties as of the immense distances which separate them from Britain, and have made interference by her impracticable. The most explicit guarantees, including the Dominions' acknowledged right to secede, would be necessary to secure for Ireland an equal degree of freedom. There is no suggestion, however, in the proposals made of any such guarantees. Instead, the natural position is reversed; our geographical situation with respect to Britain is made the basis of denials and restrictions unheard of in the case of the Dominions; the smaller island must give military safeguards and guarantees to the larger and suffer itself to be reduced to the position of a helpless dependency.

It should be obvious that we could not urge the acceptance of such proposals upon our people. A certain treaty of free association with the British Commonwealth group, as with a partial League of Nations, we would have been ready to recommend, and as a Government to negotiate and take responsibility for, had we an assurance that the entry of the nation as a whole into such association would secure for it the allegiance of the present dissenting minority, to meet whose sentiment alone this step could be contemplated.

Treaties dealing with the proposals for free intertrade and mutual limitation of armaments we are ready at any time to negotiate. Mutual agreement for facilitating air communications, as well as railway and other communications, can we feel certain also be effected. No obstacle of any kind will be placed by us in the way of that smooth commercial intercourse which is essential in the life of both islands, each the best customer and the best market of the other. It must of course be understood that all treaties and agreements would have to be submitted for ratification to the National Legislature in the first instance, and subsequently to the Irish people as a whole, under circumstances which would make it evident that their decision would be a free decision, and that every element of military compulsion was absent.

The question of Ireland's liability "for a share of the present debt of the United Kingdom" we are prepared to leave to be determined by a board of arbitrators, one appointed by Ireland, one by Great

Britain, and a third to be chosen by agreement, or in default, to be nominated, say by the President of the United States of America, if the President would consent.

As regards the question at issue between the political minority and the great majority of the Irish people, that must remain a question for the Irish people themselves to settle. We cannot admit the right of the British Government to mutilate our country, either in its own interest or at the call of any section of our population. We do not contemplate the use of force. If your Government stands aside, we can effect a complete reconciliation. We agree with you "that no common action can be secured by force." Our regret is that this wise and true principle which your Government prescribes to us for the settlement of our local problem it seems unwilling to apply consistently to the fundamental problem of the relations between our island and yours. The principle we rely on in the one case we are ready to apply in the other, but should this principle not yield an immediate settlement we are willing that this question too be submitted to external arbitration.

Thus we are ready to meet you in all that is reasonable and just. The responsibility for initiating and effecting an honourable peace rests primarily not with our Government but with yours. We have no conditions to impose, no claims to advance but the one, that we be freed from aggression. We reciprocate with a sincerity to be measured only by the terrible sufferings our people have undergone the desire you express for mutual and lasting friendship. The sole cause of the "ancient feuds" which you deplore has been, as we know, and as history proves, the attacks of English rulers upon Irish liberties. These attacks can cease forthwith, if your Government has the will. The road to peace and understanding lies open.

I am, Sir,
Faithfully yours,
EAMON DE VALERA

The Prime Minister's reply to Mr de Valera's letter of 10th August, 1921

10, *Downing Street*

Sir,   13*th August*, 1921

The earlier part of your letter is so much opposed to
our fundamental position that we feel bound to leave
you in no doubt of our meaning. You state that after
consulting your colleagues you confirm your declaration that our proposals are such as Dail Eireann could
not, and the Irish people would not, accept. You add
that the outline given in our draft is self-contradictory, and the principle of the pact offered to you not

easy to determine. We desire, therefore, to make our position absolutely clear.

In our opinion, nothing is to be gained by prolonging a theoretical discussion of the national status which you may be willing to accept as compared with that of the great self-governing Dominions of the British Commonwealth, but we must direct your attention to one point upon which you lay some emphasis, and upon which no British Government can compromise, namely, the claim that we should acknowledge the right of Ireland to secede from her allegiance to the King. No such right can ever be acknowledged by us. The geographical propinquity of Ireland to the British Isles is a fundamental fact. The history of the two islands for many centuries, however it is read, is sufficient proof that their destinies are indissolubly linked. Ireland has sent members to the British Parliament for more than a hundred years. Many thousands of her people have enlisted freely and served gallantly in the forces of the Crown. Great numbers in all the Irish provinces are profoundly attached to the Throne. These facts permit of one answer, and one only, to the claim that Britain should negotiate with Ireland as a separate and foreign Power.

When you, as the chosen representative of Irish national ideals, came to speak with me, I made one condition only, of which our proposals plainly stated the effect—that Ireland should recognise the force of geographical and historical facts. It is those facts which govern the problem of British and Irish relations. If they did not exist, there would be no problem to discuss.

I pass therefore to the conditions which are imposed by these facts. We set them out clearly in six clauses in our former proposals, and need not restate them here, except to say that the British Government cannot consent to the reference of any such questions, which concern Great Britain and Ireland alone, to the arbitration of a foreign Power.

We are profoundly glad to have your agreement that Northern Ireland cannot be coerced. This point is of great importance, because the resolve of our people to resist with their full power any attempt at secession by one part of Ireland carries with it of necessity an equal resolve to resist any effort to coerce another part of Ireland to abandon its allegiance to the Crown. We gladly give you the assurance that we will concur in any settlement which Southern and Northern Ireland may make for Irish unity within the six conditions already laid down, which apply to Southern and Northern Ireland alike, but we cannot agree to refer the question of your relations with Northern Ireland to foreign arbitration.

The conditions of the proposed settlement do not arise from any desire to force our will upon people of another race, but from facts which are as vital to Ireland's welfare as to our own. They contain no derogation from Ireland's status as a Dominion, no desire for British ascendancy over Ireland, and no impairment of Ireland's national ideals.

Our proposals present to the Irish people an opportunity such as has never dawned in their history before. We have made them in the sincere desire to achieve peace; but beyond them we cannot go. We trust that you will be able to accept them in principle. I shall be ready to discuss their application in detail whenever your acceptance in principle is communicated to me.

I am,
Yours faithfully,
D. LLOYD GEORGE

Mr de Valera's reply to the Prime Minister's letter of 13th August, 1921
(Official translation)

Mansion House, Dublin

Sir,   10*th August,* 1921

The anticipatory judgment I gave in my reply of the 10th August has been confirmed. I laid the proposals of your Government before Dail Eireann, and, by an unanimous vote, it has rejected them.

From your letter of the 13th August it was clear that the principle we were asked to accept was that the "geographical propinquity" of Ireland to Britain imposed the condition of the subordination of Ireland's right to Britain's strategic interests as she conceives them, and that the very length and persistence of the efforts made in the past to compel Ireland's acquiescence in a foreign domination imposed the condition of acceptance of that domination now.

We cannot believe that your Government intended to commit itself to a principle of sheer militarism destructive of international morality and fatal to the world's peace. If a small nation's right to independence is forfeit when a more powerful neighbour covets its territory for the military or other advantages it is supposed to confer, there is an end to liberty. No longer can any small nation claim a right to a separate sovereign existence. Holland and Denmark can be made subservient to Germany, Belgium to Germany or to France, Portugal to Spain. If nations that have been forcibly annexed to empires lose thereby their title to independence, there can be for them no rebirth to freedom. In Ireland's case, to speak of her seceding from a partnership she has not accepted, or from an allegiance which she has not undertaken to render, is fundamentally false, just as the claim to subordinate her independence to British strategy is fundamentally unjust. To neither can we, as the representatives of the nation, lend countenance.

If our refusal to betray our nation's honour and the trust that has been reposed in us is to be made an issue of war by Great Britain, we deplore it. We are as conscious of our responsibilities to the living as we are mindful of principle or of our obligations to the heroic dead. We have not sought war, nor do we seek war, but if war be made upon us we must defend ourselves and shall do so, confident that whether our defence be successful or unsuccessful no body of representative Irishmen or Irishwomen will ever propose to the nation the surrender of its birthright.

We long to end the conflict between Britain and Ireland. If your Government be determined to impose its will upon us by force and, antecedent to negotiation, to insist upon conditions that involve a surrender of our whole national position and make negotiation a mockery, the responsibility for the continuance of the conflict rests upon you.

On the basis of the broad guiding principle of government by the consent of the governed, peace can be secured—a peace that will be just and honourable to all, and fruitful of concord and enduring amity. To negotiate such a peace, Dail Eireann is ready to appoint its representatives, and, if your Government accepts the principle proposed, to invest them with plenary powers to meet and arrange with you for its application in detail.

I am, Sir,
Faithfully yours,
EAMON DE VALERA

The Prime Minister's reply to Mr de Valera's letter of 24th August, 1921

       10, *Downing Street, London, SW1*

Sir,   26th *August*,1921

The British Government are profoundly disappointed by your letter of the 24th August, which was delivered to me yesterday. You write of the conditions of a meeting between us as though no meeting had ever taken place. I must remind you, therefore, that when I asked you to meet me six weeks ago, I made no pre-liminary conditions of any sort. You came to London on that invitation and exchanged views with me at three meetings of considerable length. The proposals which I made to you after those meetings were based upon full and sympathetic consideration of the views which you expressed. As I have already said, they were not made in any haggling spirit. On the contrary, my colleagues and I went to the very limit of our powers in endeavouring to reconcile British and Irish interests. Our proposals have gone far beyond all precedent, and have been approved as liberal by the whole civilised world. Even in quarters which have shown a sympathy with the most extreme of Irish claims, they are regarded as the utmost which the Empire can reasonably offer or Ireland reasonably expect. The only criticism of them which I have yet heard outside Ireland is from those who maintain that our proposals have outstepped both warrant and wisdom in their liberality. Your letter shows no recognition of this, and further negotiations must, I fear, be futile unless some definite progress is made towards acceptance of a basis.

You declare that our proposals involve a surrender of Ireland's whole national position and reduce her to subservience. What are the facts? Under the settlement which we have outlined Ireland would control every nerve and fibre of her national existence; she would speak her own language and make her own religious life; she would have complete power over taxation and finance, subject only to an agreement for keeping trade and transport as free as possible between herself and Great Britain, her best market; she would have uncontrolled authority over education and all the moral and spiritual interests of her race; she would have it also over law and order, over land and agriculture, over the conditions of labour and industry, over the health and homes of her people, and over her own land defence. She would, in fact, within the shores of Ireland, be free in every aspect of national activity, national expression and national development. The States of the American Union, sovereign though they be, enjoy no such range of rights. And our proposals go even further, for they invite Ireland to take her place as a partner in the great commonwealth of free nations united by allegiance to the King.

We consider that these proposals completely fulfil your wish that the principle of "government by consent of the governed" should be the broad guiding principle of the settlement which your plenipotentiaries are to negotiate. That principle was first developed in England, and is the mainspring of the representative institutions which she was the first to create. It was spread by her throughout the world, and is now the very life of the British Commonwealth. We could not have invited the Irish people to take their place in that Commonwealth on any other principle, and we are convinced that through it we can heal the old misunderstandings and achieve an enduring partnership as honourable to Ireland as to the other nations of which the Commonwealth consists.

But when you argue that the relations of Ireland with the British Empire are comparable in principle to those of Holland or Belgium with the German Empire, I find it necessary to repeat once more that those are premises which no British Government, whatever its complexion, can ever accept. In demanding that Ireland should be treated as a separate sovereign Power, with no allegiance to the Crown and no loyalty to the sister nations of the Commonwealth, you are advancing claims which the most famous national leaders in Irish history, from Grattan to Parnell and Redmond, have explicitly disowned. Grattan, in a famous phrase, declared that "the ocean protests against separation, and the sea against union." Daniel O'Connell, the most eloquent perhaps of all the spokesmen of the Irish national cause, protested thus in the House of Commons in 1830:

> Never did monarch receive more undivided
> allegiance than the present King from the men who
> in Ireland agitate the repeal of the Union. Never, too
> was there a grosser calumny than to assert that they
> wish to produce a separation between the two
> countries. Never was there a greater mistake than to
> suppose that we wish to dissolve the connection.

And in a well-known letter to the Duke of Wellington in 1845, Thomas Davis, the fervent exponent of the ideals of Young Ireland, wrote:

> I do not seek a raw repeal of the Act of Union. I
> want you to retain the Imperial Parliament with its
> Imperial power. I ask you only to disencumber it of

those cares which exhaust its patience and embarrass its attention. I ask you to give Ireland a Senate of some sort, selected by the people, in part or in whole; levying their Customs and Excise and other taxes; making their roads, harbours, railways, canals, and bridges; encouraging their manufactures, commerce, agriculture and fisheries; settling their Poor Laws, their tithes, tenures, grand juries and franchises; giving a vent to ambition, an opportunity for knowledge, restoring the absentees, securing work, and diminishing poverty, crime, ignorance and discontent. This, were I an Englishman, I should ask for England, besides the Imperial Parliament. So would I for Wales, were I a Welshman, and for Scotland, were I a Scotchman; this I ask for Ireland.

The British Government have offered Ireland all that O'Connell and Thomas Davis asked, and more; and we are met only by an unqualified demand that we should recognise Ireland as a foreign Power. It is playing with phrases to suggest that the principle of government by consent of the governed compels a recognition of that demand on our part, or that in repudiating it we are straining geographical and historical considerations to justify a claim to ascendency over the Irish race. There is no political principle, however clear, that can be applied without regard to limitations imposed by physical and historical facts. Those limitations are as necessary as the very principle itself to the structure of every free nation; to deny them would involve the dissolution of all democratic

States. It is on these elementary grounds that we have called attention to the governing force of the geographical propinquity of these two islands, and of their long historic association despite great differences of character and race. We do not believe that the permanent reconciliation of Great Britain and Ireland can ever be attained without a recognition of their physical and historical interdependence, which makes complete political and economic separation impracticable for both.

I cannot better express the British standpoint in this respect than in words used of the Northern and Southern States by Abraham Lincoln in the First Inaugural Address. They were spoken by him on the brink of the American Civil War, which he was striving to avert:

> Physically speaking we cannot separate. We cannot remove our respective sections from each other, nor build an impassable wall between them. . . . It is impossible, then, to make that intercourse more advantageous or more satisfactory after separation than before. . . . Suppose you go to war, you cannot fight always; and when, after much loss on both sides and no gain on either, you cease fighting, the identical old questions as to terms of intercourse are again upon you.

I do not think it can be reasonably contended that the relations of Great Britain and Ireland are in any different case.

I thought I had made it clear, both in my conversations with you and in my two subsequent communications, that we can discuss no settlement which involves a refusal on the part of Ireland to accept our invitation to free, equal, and loyal partnership in the British Commonwealth under one Sovereign. We are reluctant to precipitate the issue, but we must point out that a prolongation of the present state of affairs is dangerous. Action is being taken in various directions which, if continued, would prejudice the truce and must ultimately lead to its termination. This would indeed be deplorable. Whilst, therefore, prepared to make every allowance as to time which will advance the cause of peace, we cannot prolong a mere exchange of notes. It is essential that some definite and immediate progress should be made towards a basis upon which further negotiations can usefully proceed. Your letter seems to us unfortunately to show no such progress.

In this and my previous letters I have set forth the considerations which must govern the attitude of His Majesty's Government in any negotiations which they undertake. If you are prepared to examine how far these considerations can be reconciled with the aspirations which you represent, I shall be happy to meet you and your colleagues.

I am, Sir,
Yours faithfully,
D. LLOYD GEORGE

Reply received from Mr de Valera, 31st August, 1921
(Official translation)

                                    Mansion House, Dublin
Sir,   30*th August*, 1921
We, too, are convinced that it is essential that some
"definite and immediate progress should be made
towards a basis upon which further negotiations can
usefully proceed", and recognise the futility of a
"mere exchange" of argumentative notes. I shall
therefore refrain from commenting on the fallacious
historical references in your last communication. The
present is the reality with which we have to deal. The

conditions to-day are the resultant of the past, accurately summing it up and giving in simplest form the essential data of the problem. These data are:

1. The people of Ireland, acknowledging no voluntary union with Great Britain, and claiming as a fundamental natural right to choose freely for themselves the path they shall take to realise their national destiny, have, by an overwhelming majority, declared for independence, set up a republic and more than once confirmed their choice.

2. Great Britain, on the other hand, acts as though Ireland were bound to her by a contract of union that forbade separation. The circumstances of the supposed contract are notorious, yet, on the theory of its validity, the British Government and Parliament claim to rule and legislate for Ireland, even to the point of partitioning Irish territory against the will of the Irish people, and killing or casting into prison every Irish citizen who refuses allegiance.

The proposals of your Government, submitted in the draft of the 20th July, are based fundamentally on the latter premises. We have rejected these proposals, and our rejection is irrevocable. They were *not* an invitation to Ireland to enter into "a free and willing" partnership with the free nations of the British Commonwealth. They were an invitation to Ireland to enter in a guise and under conditions which determine a status definitely inferior to that of these free

States. Canada, Australia, South Africa, New Zealand are all guaranteed against the domination of the major State, not only by the acknowledged constitutional rights which give them equality of status with Great Britain and absolute freedom from the control of the British Parliament and Government, but by the thousands of miles that separate them from Great Britain. Ireland would have the guarantees neither of distance nor of right. The condition sought to be imposed would divide her into two artificial States, each destructive of the other's influence in any common council, and both subject to the military, naval and economic control of the British Government.

The main historical and geographical facts are not in dispute, but your Government insists on viewing them from your standpoint. We must be allowed to view them from ours. The history that you interpret as dictating union we read as dictating separation. Our interpretations of the fact of "geographical propinquity" are no less diametrically opposed. We are convinced that ours is the true and just interpretation, and, as a proof, are willing that a neutral, impartial arbitrator should be the judge. You refuse, and threaten to give effect to your view by force. Our reply must be that if you adopt that course we can only resist, as the generations before us have resisted.

Force will not solve the problem. It will never secure the ultimate victory over reason and right. If you again resort to force, and if victory be not on the side of justice, the problem that confronts us will confront our successors. The fact that for 750 years this problem has resisted a solution by force is evidence and warning sufficient. It is true wisdom, therefore, and true statesmanship, not any false idealism, that prompts me and my colleagues. Threats of force must be set aside. They must be set aside from the beginning, as well as during the actual conduct of the negotiations. The respective plenipotentiaries must meet untrammelled by any conditions save the facts themselves, and must be prepared to reconcile their subsequent differences not by appeals to force, covert or open, but by reference to some guiding principle on which there is common agreement. We have proposed the principle of government by the consent of the governed, and do not mean it as a mere phrase. It is a simple expression of the test to which any proposed solution must respond if it is to prove adequate, and it can be used as a criterion for the details as well as for the whole. That you claim as a peculiarly British principle, instituted by Britain, and "now the very life of the British Commonwealth" should make it peculiarly acceptable to you. On this basis and this only we see a hope of reconciling "the considerations which must govern the attitude" of Britain's representatives with the considerations that must govern the attitude of Ireland's representatives, and on this basis we are ready at once to appoint plenipotentiaries.

I am, Sir,

Faithfully yours,

EAMON DE VALERA

⚬⚬⊱⊰⚬⚬

The Prime Minister's reply to Mr de Valera's letter of 30th August, 1921

Town Hall, Inverness

Sir, 7th September, 1921

His Majesty's Government have considered your letter of the 30th August, and have to make the following observations upon it:

The principle of government by consent of the governed is the foundation of British constitutional development, but we cannot accept as a basis of practical conference an interpretation of that principle which would commit us to any demands which you might present—even to the extent of setting up a Republic and repudiating the Crown. You must be aware that conference on such a basis is impossible. So applied, the principle of government by consent of the governed would undermine the fabric of every democratic State and drive the civilised world back into tribalism.

On the other hand, we have invited you to discuss our proposals on their merits, in order that you may have no doubt as to the scope and sincerity of our intentions. It would be open to you in such a conference to raise the subject of guarantees on any points in which you may consider Irish freedom prejudiced by these proposals.

His Majesty's Government are loth to believe that you will insist upon rejecting their proposals without examining them in conference. To decline to discuss a settlement which would bestow upon the Irish people the fullest freedom of national development within the Empire can only mean that you repudiate all allegiance to the Crown and all membership of the British Commonwealth. If we were to draw this inference from your letter, then further discussion between us could serve no useful purpose, and all conference would be vain. If, however, we are mistaken in this inference, as we still hope, and if your real objection to our proposals is that they offer Ireland less than the liberty which we have described, that objection can be explored at a conference.

You will agree that this correspondence has lasted long enough. His Majesty's Government must, there-

fore, ask for a definite reply as to whether you are prepared to enter a conference to ascertain how the
association of Ireland with the community of nations
known as the British Empire can best be reconciled
with Irish national aspirations. If, as we hope, your
answer is in the affirmative, I suggest that the conference should meet at Inverness on the 20th instant.

I am, Sir,
Yours faithfully,
D. Lloyd George

Reply received from Mr de Valera, 13th September, 1921
(Official translation)

Mansion House, Dublin

Sir,   12*th September,* 1921

We have no hesitation in declaring our willingness to
enter a conference to ascertain how the association of
Ireland with the community of nations known as the
British Empire can best be reconciled with Irish
national aspirations. Our readiness to contemplate
such an association was indicated in our letter of the
10th August. We have accordingly summoned Dail
Eireann that we may submit to it for ratification the

names of the representatives it is our intention to propose. We hope that these representatives will find it possible to be at Inverness on the date you suggest, the 20th September.

In this final note we deem it our duty to reaffirm that our position is and can only be as we have defined it throughout this correspondence. Our nation has formally declared its independence and recognises itself as a sovereign State. It is only as the representatives of that State and as its chosen guardians that we have any authority or powers to act on behalf of our people.

As regards the principle of "government by consent of the governed", in the very nature of things it must be the basis of any agreement that will achieve the purpose we have at heart, that is, the final reconciliation of our nation with yours. We have suggested no interpretation of that principle save its every day interpretation—the sense, for example, in which it was understood by the plain men and women of the world when on the 5th January, 1918, you said:

> The settlement of the New Europe must be based on such grounds of reason and justice as will give some promise of stability. Therefore it is that we feel that government with the consent of the governed must be the basis of any territorial settlement in this war.

These words are the true answer to the criticism of our position which your last letter puts forward. The principle was understood then to mean the right of nations that had been annexed to empires against their will to free themselves from the grappling hook. That is the sense in which we understood it. In reality it is your Government, when it seeks to rend our ancient nation and to partition its territory, that would give to the principle an interpretation that "would undermine the fabric of every democratic State, and drive the civilised world back into tribalism."

EAMON DE VALERA

The Prime Minister's reply to Mr de Valera's letter of 12th September, 1921

(Telegraphed)

Sir,   15th September, 1921

I informed your emissaries who came to me here on Tuesday, the 13th, that the reiteration of your claim to negotiate with His Majesty's Government as the representatives of an independent and sovereign State would make conference between us impossible. They brought me a letter from you in which you specifically reaffirm that claim, stating that your nation "has formally declared its independence and recognises itself as a sovereign State," and "it is only," you added, "as the representatives of that State, and as its chosen guardians, that we have any authority or powers to act on behalf of our people." I asked them to warn you of the very serious effects of such a paragraph, and I offered to regard the letter as undelivered to me in order that you might have time to reconsider it.

Despite this intimation, you have now published the letter in its original form. I must accordingly cancel the arrangements for conference next week at Inverness, and must consult my colleagues on the course of action which this new situation necessitates. I will communicate this to you as soon as possible, but, as I am for the moment laid up here, a few days' delay is inevitable.

Meanwhile, I must make it absolutely clear that His Majesty's Government cannot reconsider the position which I have stated to you. If we accepted conference with your delegates on a formal statement of the claim which you have reaffirmed, it would constitute an official recognition by His Majesty's Government of the severance of Ireland from the Empire and of its existence as an independent Republic. It would, moreover, entitle you to declare as of right acknowledged by us that in preference to association with the British Empire you would pursue a closer association by treaty with some foreign Power. There is only one answer possible to such a claim as that.

The great concessions which His Majesty's Government have made to the feeling of your people in order to secure a lasting settlement deserve, in my opinion, some more generous response, but, so far, every advance has been made by us. On your part you have not come to meet us by a single step, but have merely reiterated in phrases of emphatic challenge the letter and spirit of your original claim.

I am,
Yours faithfully,
D. Lloyd George

Reply received from Mr de Valera, 16th September, 1921
(Telegraphed)

Sir,   16*th September*, 1921

I received your telegram last night. I am surprised that you do not see that if we on our side accepted the conference on the basis of your letter of the 7th September without making our position equally clear, Ireland's representatives would enter the conference with their position misunderstood and the cause of Ireland's right irreparably prejudiced. Throughout the correspondence that has taken place you have defined your Government's position. We have defined ours. If the positions were not so definitely opposed there would indeed be no problem to discuss. It should be obvious that in a case like this if there is to be any result the negotiators must meet without prejudice and untrammelled by any conditions whatsoever, except those imposed by the facts as they know them.

EAMON DE VALERA

The Prime Minister's reply to Mr de Valera's letter of 16th September, 1921
(Telegraphed)

Gairloch

Sir,   17*th September*, 1921

I have received the communication which you telegraphed to me last night.

It is idle to say that a conference in which we had already met your delegates as representatives of an independent and sovereign State would be a conference "without prejudice". To receive them as such would constitute a formal and official recognition of

Ireland's severance from the King's domains. It would indeed entitle you, if you thought fit, to make a treaty of amity with the King, but it would equally entitle you to make no treaty at all, to break off the conference with us at any period, and, by a right which we ourselves had already recognised, to negotiate the union of Ireland with a foreign Power. It would also entitle you, if you insisted upon another appeal to force, to claim from foreign Powers, by our implicit admission, the rights of lawful belligerents against the King; if we dealt with you as a sovereign and independent State we should have no right to complain of other Powers for following our example. These would be the consequences of receiving your delegates as representatives of an independent State. We are prepared, in the words of my letter of the 7th, to discuss with you "How the association of Ireland with the community of nations known as the British Empire can best be reconciled with Irish national aspirations."

We cannot consent to any abandonment, however informal, of the principle of allegiance to the King, upon which the whole fabric of the Empire and every Constitution within it are based. It is fatal to that principle that your delegates in the conference should be there as the representatives of an independent and sovereign State. While you insist on claiming that, conference between us is impossible.

I am,
Yours faithfully,
D. LLOYD GEORGE

Reply received from Mr de Valera, 17th September, 1921
(Telegraphed)

Mansion House, Dublin
Sir,   17*th September,* 1921
In reply to your last telegram just received, I have
only to say that we have already accepted your invitation in the exact words which you re-quote from
your letter of the 7th instant. We have not asked you
to abandon any principle, even informally, but surely
you must understand that we can only recognise ourselves for what we are. If this self-recognition be made

a reason for the cancellation of the conference, we regret it, but it seems inconsistent.

I have already had conferences with you, and in these conferences and in my written communications I have never ceased to recognise myself for what I was and am. If this involves recognition on your part, then you have already recognised us. Had it been our desire to add to the solid substance of Ireland's right the veneer of the technicalities of international usage which you now introduce we might have claimed already the advantage of all these consequences which you fear would flow from the reception of our delegates now. Believe me, we have but one object at heart—the setting of the conference on such a basis of truth and reality as would make it possible to secure through it the result which the people of these two islands so ardently desire.

I am, Sir,

Yours faithfully,

EAMON DE VALERA

The Prime Minister's reply to Mr de Valera's letter of 17th September, 1921
(Telegraphed)

Gairloch

Sir,   18*th September*, 1921
I have received your telegram of last night, and observe that it does not modify the claim that your delegates should meet us as the representatives of a sovereign and independent State.

You made no such condition in advance when you came to see me in July. I invited you then to meet me, in the words of my letter, as "the chosen leader of the great majority in Southern Ireland", and you accepted that invitation. From the very outset of our conversations I told you that we looked to Ireland to own allegiance to the Throne, and to make her future as a member of the British Commonwealth. That was the basis of our proposals, and we cannot alter it. The status which you now claim in advance for your delegates is in effect a repudiation of that basis.

I am prepared to meet your delegates, as I met you in July, in the capacity of "chosen spokesmen" for your people to discuss the association of Ireland with the British Commonwealth. My colleagues and I cannot meet them as the representatives of a sovereign and independent State without disloyalty on our part to the Throne and the Empire. I must, therefore, repeat that, unless the second paragraph in your letter of the 12th is withdrawn, conference between us is impossible.

I am,
Yours faithfully,
D. LLOYD GEORGE

Reply received from Mr de Valera, 19th September, 1921
(Telegraphed)

Mansion House, Dublin,

Sir, 19*th September*, 1921

We have had no thought at any time of asking you to accept any conditions precedent to a conference. We would have thought it as unreasonable to expect you as a preliminary to recognise the Irish Republic formally or informally as that you should expect us formally or informally to surrender our national position. It is precisely because neither side accepts the position of the other that there is a dispute at all, and that a conference is necessary to search for and discuss such adjustments as might compose it.

A treaty of accommodation and association properly concluded between the peoples of these two islands and between Ireland and the group of States in the British Commonwealth would, we believe, end the dispute for ever and enable the two nations to settle down in peace, each pursuing its own individual development and contributing its own quota to civilisation, but working together in free and friendly co-operation in affairs of agreed common concern. To negotiate such a treaty the respective representatives of the two nations must meet. If you seek to impose preliminary conditions which we must regard as involving a surrender of our whole position they cannot meet.

Your last telegram makes it clear that misunderstandings are more likely to increase than to diminish, and the cause of peace more likely to be retarded than advanced by a continuance of the present correspondence. We request you, therefore, to state whether your letter of the 7th September is intended to be a demand for a surrender on our part or an invitation to a conference free on both sides, and without prejudice should agreement not be reached. If the latter we readily confirm our acceptance of the invitation, and our appointed delegates will meet your Government's representatives at any time in the immediate future that you designate.

I am, Sir,
Yours faithfully,
EAMON DE VALERA

The Prime Minister's reply to Mr de Valera's letter of 19th September, 1921
(Telegraphed)

Gairloch

Sir,   *29th September,* 1921

His Majesty's Government have given close and earnest consideration to the correspondence which has passed between us since their invitation to you to send delegates to a conference at Inverness. In spite of their sincere desire for peace, and in spite of the more conciliatory tone of your last communication, they cannot enter a conference upon the basis of this correspondence. Notwithstanding your personal assurance to the contrary, which they much appreciate, it might be argued in future that the acceptance of a conference on this basis had involved them in a recognition which no British Government can accord. On this point they must guard themselves against any possible doubt. There is no purpose to be served by any further interchange of explanatory and argumentative communications upon this subject. The position taken up by His Majesty's Government is fundamental to the existence of the British Empire, and they cannot alter it. My colleagues and I remain, however, keenly anxious to make, in co-operation with your delegates, another determined effort to explore every possibility of settlement by personal discussion. The proposals which we have already made have been taken by the whole world as proof that our endeavours for reconciliation and settlement are no empty form; and we feel that conference, not correspondence, is the most practical and hopeful way to an understanding such as we ardently desire to achieve. We therefore send herewith a fresh invitation to a conference in London on the 11th October, where we can meet your delegates as spokesmen of the people whom you represent, with a view to ascertaining how the association of Ireland with the community of nations known as the British Empire may best be reconciled with Irish national aspirations.

I am, Sir,

Yours faithfully,

D. Lloyd George

Reply received from Mr de Valera, 30th September, 1921
(Telegraphed)

Dublin

Sir,   *30th September,* 1921

We have received your letter of invitation to a conference in London on the 11th October, "with a view to ascertaining how the association of Ireland with the community of nations known as the British Empire may best be reconciled with Irish national aspirations."

Our respective positions have been stated and are understood, and we agree that conference, not correspondence, is the most practical and hopeful way to an understanding. We accept the invitation and our delegates will meet you in London on the date mentioned "to explore every possibility of settlement by personal discussion."

Faithfully yours,

EAMON DE VALERA

Other titles in the series

The Amritsar Massacre: General Dyer in the Punjab, 1919

"We feel that General Dyer, by adopting an inhuman and un-British method of dealing with subjects of His Majesty the King-Emperor, has done great disservice to the interest of British rule in India. This aspect it was not possible for the people of the mentality of General Dyer to realise."

Backdrop

At the time of the events described, India was under British rule. Indians had fought alongside the British in World War I, and had made tremendous financial contributions to the British war effort. Mahatma Gandhi was the leader of the Indian National Congress party, which was seeking independence from the British Empire.

The Book

This is the story of the action taken by Brigadier-General Dyer at Amritsar in the Punjab in 1919. Faced with insurrection in support of Mahatma Gandhi, the British Army attempted to restore order. General Dyer, on arriving in the troubled city of Amritsar, issued an order banning any assembly of more than four people. Consequently, when he discovered a large crowd gathered together during a cattle fair, he took the astonishing action of shooting more than three hundred unarmed people. Regarding the subsequent native obedience as a satisfactory result, he was surprised to find himself removed from command a year later, and made lengthy representations to Parliament.

ISBN 0 11 702412 0   Price £6.99

British Battles of World War I, 1914–15

"The effect of these poisonous gases was so virulent as to render the whole of the line held by the French Division incapable of any action at all. It was at first impossible for anyone to realise what had actually happened. The smoke and fumes hid everything from sight, and hundreds of men were thrown into a comatose or dying condition, and within an hour the whole position had to be abandoned, together with about 50 guns."

Backdrop

On 4 August 1914, Britain declared war on Germany. Germany had already invaded Belgium and France and was progressing towards Paris.

The Book

These are the despatches from some of the battles of the first two years of World War I. They include action in northern France, Germany, Gallipoli, and even as far afield as the Cocos Islands in the Indian Ocean. They describe the events of battle, the tremendous courage, the huge losses, and the confusions and difficulties of war. These startling accounts, which were written by the generals at the front, were first published in the "London Gazette", the official newspaper of Parliament.

ISBN 0 11 702447 3   Price £6.99

Florence Nightingale and the Crimea, 1854–55

*"By an oversight, no candles were included among the stores brought to
the Crimea. Lamps and wicks were brought but not oil. These omissions
were not supplied until after possession had been taken of Balaklava,
and the purveyor had an opportunity of purchasing candles and oil from
the shipping and the dealers in the town."*

Backdrop

The British Army arrived in the Crimea in 1854, ill-equipped
to fight a war in the depths of a Russian winter.

The Book

The hospital service for wounded soldiers during the Crimean
War was very poor and became the subject of concern, not just
in the army, but also in the press. "The Times" was publishing
letters from the families of soldiers describing the appalling conditions. This embarrassed the government, but even more it
irritated the army, which did not know how to cope with such
open scrutiny of its activities.

The book is a collection of extracts from government
papers published in 1855 and 1856. Their selection provides a
snapshot of events at that time. In particular they focus on the
terrible disaster that was the Charge of the Light Brigade, and
the inadequate provisions that were made for the care of the sick
and wounded. The documents relating to the hospitals at Scutari
include evidence from Florence Nightingale herself.

ISBN 0 11 702425 2   Price £6.99

Lord Kitchener and Winston Churchill: The Dardanelles Commission Part I, 1914–15

"The naval attack on the Narrows was never resumed. It is difficult to understand why the War Council did not meet between 19th March and 14th May. The failure of the naval attack showed the necessity of abandoning the plan of forcing the passage of the Dardanelles by purely naval operation. The War Council should then have met and considered the future policy to be pursued."

Backdrop

The Dardanelles formed part of the main southern shipping route to Russia, and was of great military and strategic importance. However, it had long been recognised by the British naval and military authorities that any attack on the Dardanelles would be an operation fraught with great difficulties.

The Book

During the early stages of World War I, Russia made a plea to her allies to make a demonstration against the Turks. So attractive was the prize of the Dardanelles to the British generals, notably Lord Kitchener, that this ill-fated campaign was launched. Just how powerful an influence Kitchener was to exert over the War Council, and just how ill-prepared the Allies were to conduct such an attack, are revealed in dramatic detail in the report of this Commission.

The book covers the first part of the Commission's report. It deals with the origin, inception and conduct of operations in the Dardanelles from the beginning of the war in August 1914 until March 1915, when the idea of a purely naval attack was abandoned.

ISBN 0 11 702423 6   Price £6.99

The Russian Revolution, 1917

"It is the general opinion in Ekaterinburg that the Empress, her son, and four daughters were not murdered, but were despatched on the 17th July to the north or the west. The story that they were burnt in a house seems to be an exaggeration of the fact that in a wood outside the town was found a heap of ashes, apparently the result of burning a considerable amount of clothing. At the bottom of the ashes was a diamond, and, as one of the Grand Duchesses is said to have sewn a diamond into the lining of her cloak, it is supposed that the clothes of the Imperial family were burnt there."

Backdrop

By November 1917 Russia had lost more than twenty million people in the war. Lenin's Bolshevik party had overthrown the Tsar and had called for an end to all capitalist governments.

The Book

Government files contain a number of detailed documents describing the nature of the Bolshevik Revolution and the government of Lenin, which was observed to be not only abhorrent but also menacing because of the international implications. The book is compiled from two of these files, one of which describes the events leading up to the revolution and how the Bolsheviks came to power in October 1917. The other contains a series of eye-witness accounts of the frightening days of the Bolshevik regime from the summer of 1918 to April 1919.

ISBN 0 11 702424 4   Price £6.99

UFOs in the House of Lords, 1979

"Is it not time that Her Majesty's Government informed our people of what they know about UFOs? The UFOs have been coming in increasing numbers for 30 years since the war, and I think it is time our people were told the truth. We have not been invaded from outer space. Most incidents have not been hostile. Indeed it is us, the earthlings, who have fired on them. . . . Whatever the truth is, I am sure that an informed public is a prepared one. Another thing: it is on record that both sighting and landing reports are increasing all the time. Just suppose the 'ufonauts' decided to make mass landings tomorrow in this country—there could well be panic here, because our people have not been prepared."

Backdrop

The winter of 1978/79 in Britain was a time of strikes and unrest. It became known as the "winter of discontent". Yet it seems that the House of Lords had other more important things to discuss.

The Book

The book is the transcript of a debate in the House of Lords which took place in February 1979. Their Lordships debated the need for an international initiative in response to the problem of Unidentified Flying Objects. There were several notable speeches from noble lords and distinguished prelates.

ISBN 0 11 702413 9   Price £6.99

D Day to VE Day: General Eisenhower's Report, 1944–45

"During the spring of 1945, as the sky grew darker over Germany, the Nazi leaders had struggled desperately, by every means in their power, to whip their people into a last supreme effort to stave off defeat, hoping against hope that it would be possible, if only they could hold out long enough, to save the day by dividing the Allies. Blinded as they were by their own terror and hatred of 'Bolshevism', they were incapable of understanding the strength of the bond of common interest existing between Britain, the United States and the Soviet Union."

Backdrop
In 1944 the Allies were poised to launch an attack against Hitler's German war machine. The planning and timing were crucial. In February, General Eisenhower was appointed Supreme Commander of the Allied Operations in Europe.

The Book
The book is Dwight D. Eisenhower's personal account of the Allied invasion of Europe, from the preparations for the D-Day landings in Normandy, France, to the final assault across Germany. He presents a story of a far more arduous struggle than is commonly portrayed against an enemy whose tenacity he admired and whose skills he feared. It is a tactical account of his understanding of enemy manoeuvres, and his attempts to counter their actions. The formality of the report is coloured by many personal touches, and the reader senses Eisenhower's growing determination to complete the task. Hindsight would have had the general take more notice of Russian activity, but that this was not obvious to him is one of the fascinations of such a contemporary document.

ISBN 0 11 702451 1   Price £6.99